PRAISE FOR *THE TAPPING CURE*:

"*The Tapping Cure* is good for what ails you—a must-have for your emotional First-Aid Kit."

—PATRICIA FRENCH CRILLY, RN

"Tapping helps me overcome the anxiety that can overwhelm me at times since the loss of my husband. The tapping seems to steady me."

—H. KATZ, ED.D.
Hunter College faculty

"*The Tapping Cure* is informative, educational and on the cutting-edge of therapy. You'll want to keep the information in your pocket at all times. I know I will be referring to it often. *The Tapping Cure* has caused me to take a new look at how I might help my own patients eliminate specific symptoms."

—CAROL LEVANTROSSER, Ph.D.,
licensed clinical psychologist

 ROBERTA TEMES, PHD, is a psychotherapist, hypnotist, and faculty member at the Downstate Medical School. She is the author of many books on psychological well-being, including the best-selling *The Complete Idiot's Guide to Hypnosis*. For many years Dr. Temes wrote the popular monthly "Ask Dr. Roberta" column for *True Story* magazine, and she has been interviewed about her work in many magazines, including *Redbook, Allure, Brides, Good Housekeeping*, and many newspapers, too. She has a private practice and she regularly counsels guests at the Rancho La Puerta Health Spa, and teaches classes at The Learning Annex. Dr. Temes lives with her husband in Scotch Plains, New Jersey.

THE
Tapping
Cure

Other titles by Roberta Temes

The Complete Idiot's Guide to Hypnosis

Getting Your Life Back Together When You Have Schizophrenia

Living with an Empty Chair: A Guide Through Grief

Medical Hypnosis (editor)

THE
Tapping
Cure

*A Revolutionary System
for Rapid Relief from Phobias,
Anxieties, Post-Traumatic Stress
Disorder and More*

ROBERTA TEMES, PhD

Da Capo
LIFE
LONG

A Member of the Perseus Books Group

The Tapping Cure:
A Revolutionary System for Rapid Relief from Phobias,
Anxieties, Post-Traumatic Stress Disorder and More
Copyright © 2006 by Roberta Temes

Designed by Pauline Neuwirth, Neuwirth & Associates

Cataloging-in-Publication data for this book is available from the Library of Congress.

ISBN-13: 978-1-56924-324-4

Published by Da Capo Press
A Member of the Perseus Books Group
www.dacapopress.com

Note: The information in this book is true to the best of our knowledge. This book is intended only as an informative guide for those wishing to know more about health issues. In no way is this book intended to replace, countermand, or conflict with the advice given to you by your own physician. The ultimate decision concerning care should be made between you and your doctor. We strongly recommend you follow his or her advice. Information in this book is general and is offered with no guarantees on the part of the authors or Da Capo Press. The authors and publisher disclaim all liability in connection with the use of this book. The names and identifying details of people associated with events described in this book have been changed. Any similarity to actual persons is coincidental.

Da Capo Press Books are available at special discounts for bulk purchases in the U.S. by corporations, institutions, and other organizations. For more information, please contact the Special Markets Department at the Perseus Books Group, 2300 Chestnut Street, Suite 200, Philadelphia, PA, 19103, or call (800) 810-4145, ext. 5000, or e-mail special.markets@perseusbooks.com.

9 8 7

Disclaimer

THE INFORMATION IN this book is intended to help readers make informed decisions about their health and the health of their loved ones. It is not intended to be a substitute for treatment by, or the advice and care of, a professional health-care provider. While the author and publisher have endeavored to ensure that the information presented is accurate and up-to-date, they are not responsible for adverse effects or consequences sustained by any persons using this book.

Dedicated to the grandkids from A to Z:

Abraham, Alyssa, Benjy, Charlie, Hannah, Joe, Katie, Leah, and Zachary

We can easily forgive a child who is afraid of the dark; the real tragedy of life is when men are afraid of the light.

—Plato

Contents

Contents

Acknowledgments

WITH HEARTFELT THANKS to Janet Rosen, my extraordinary agent at Sheree Bykofsky Associates; and to Kylie Foxx and Renée Sedliar, my wonderful editors at Avalon.

Introduction

I AM NOT a *woo-woo* person. I don't like touchy-feely stuff. I am a pragmatist. Show me evidence. Show me scientific documentation. I prefer stomping around doing aerobics to moving slowly, softly, and gracefully in a tai chi class. And please don't give me breathing lessons; I've been breathing very well since birth with no instructions, thank you.

That said, here I am practically proselytizing for tapping. *Tapping*, for goodness sakes! What in the world has happened to me?

I have tried to figure out how I went astray.

It all started with one patient who came to see me in my psychotherapy practice. Ellen is an artist and a professor of art history. She has a husband and two children. She was leading a fairly uneventful, contented life until the day she happened to be driving in the wrong place at the wrong time.

Ellen was not hurt; she wasn't really in the accident at all. Nevertheless, she was traumatized. Six months later she appeared in my office saying that she *still* could hear the squealing brakes of the car in the next lane. She *still* could hear the shouts of pedestrians warning the driver of that car that a child was running into traffic. And at bedtime, whenever Ellen closed her eyes, she could *still* see that child gruesomely mangled.

When Ellen came into my office, I'd already been a therapist for decades. I knew what to do. I used traditional psychodynamic psychotherapy techniques and I used cognitive behavioral techniques, and then I used hypnosis. Ellen said the hypnosis helped; in fact, it made a big difference. But she was still suffering. She still had flashbacks; not as severe and not as often, but painful flashbacks, nevertheless.

I was starting to feel guilty. Ellen was trekking to my office, paying a hefty fee, and complying with all my instructions, yet although she had improved, she still had symptoms. I had been pondering Ellen's situation for some time when I received an advertisement for a book that offered a new cure for post-traumatic stress disorder (PTSD). Ellen clearly qualified as a sufferer, and I needed a new way to help her.

I promptly ordered the book. What arrived was a poorly written paperback whose title I cannot recall. It offered some crazy advice. It suggested that I tap on a patient's face and fingers while saying some very specific words. It suggested that I touch the patient's collarbones, too. That was too much for me. I'm not a touching type to begin with. And, after all, I'm a professional. Why would I poke around on a patient's collarbone?

Clearly this author was a kook, but because I was desperate to help Ellen, I hesitantly—very hesitantly—followed some of the advice. I didn't do the tapping; I instructed Ellen to do it to herself. And it was not easy. The instructions were complicated. But although it seemed bizarre, Ellen went along with me. I told her where to place her fingertips and what to say while she drummed herself. I was reading from my notes.

Within ten minutes, Ellen was smiling. She said, "What kind of hocus-pocus is this? I feel no pain when I think about the severely wounded child, and best of all, my mind doesn't go there. I can't really think about it even when I try to. Instead I'm thinking that that was in the past. That was then. This is now. The tragedy is over. I need to get on with my life."

Ellen's success motivated my own journey. I read everything I could find about the tapping phenomenon. I attended seminars, conferences, and workshops and scheduled meetings with the gurus in the field. I then introduced tapping to many of my psychotherapy clients. It was not appropriate for all of them, but for many the change was revolutionary.

After many years of working with this process, I began to shape my version of it. My opinions differed from those of some of the known experts and I added my own touch in certain areas. But best of all was my realization that folks could do it without me. They didn't need to come to my office. In one phone call, they could tell me what their situation was and I could tell them how to tap.

Even though I saw many patients helped by tapping, I still had many questions. After all, the method was not scientific; it had not been approved by the medical establishment. It certainly was not adding to my credentials as a scholar. Yet there was one very important fact I could not deny: it was working.

Next, I began to conduct tapping sessions via e-mail. After ten to fifteen minutes of tapping, most of my clients reported that they were cured. Not quite believing them, I followed up. Week after week I called. Week after week they told me they were just fine, thank you. To my astonishment, their symptoms did not return. I was amazed.

Now, after years of watching my clients heal themselves, I am determined to share the Tapping Cure with you. By now I've worked with enough tapping clients to come up with some ideas that can help almost everyone. I'd like you to be able to cure yourself. You can, you know. You truly can get rid of your symptoms.

I invite you to share my adventure. Reading this entire book will give you a good grasp of the Tapping Cure. But you will also do fine if you read only the first three chapters and then choose the chapter that relates to your situation. Go on to chapter 4 if you have a phobia. Chapter 5 will help with issues at work or if you have low self-esteem. Read chapter 6 if you need help with relationships; chapter 7 is a must for you if you're suffering from the aftereffects of a traumatic experience. If you're a parent, please go directly to chapter 9; you'll derive an immediate benefit. Once you get the hang of tapping, go to chapter 8 for interesting ideas about how to adjust your tapping techniques.

Every chapter has sidebars: Hot Spots are quick reminders of particular tapping spots for specific situations. True Reports are testimonials from my clients who have experienced the Tapping Cure themselves. Wise Words are relevant quotations from people of note.

Each chapter has a few sentences at its end under the heading Remember This. Please do read that last paragraph of each chapter; it provides an important summary as well as additional tips for successful tapping.

Although I've just advised you to read only the chapters pertaining to your circumstances, please know that I truly hope you'll read every word of *The Tapping Cure*. I wrote this book to help you and to heal you, and also to entertain you. You'll find interesting stories when you peek into my office and meet my clients. Enjoy!

What Is
the Tapping Cure?

THE TAPPING CURE is a way for you to completely erase painful feelings. It takes only a few minutes, and it requires neither medication nor talk therapy. It's an astonishing, sometimes unbelievable, method of self-help.

JENNIFER'S PHOBIA

JEN IS A typical client. She thinks tapping sounds bizarre, but she is desperate, so she agrees to come to my office and try it. Jen has a phobia that is getting in the way of her life. She explains: "I guess you could say I've always been high-strung and somewhat fearful. But until recently the things I was scared of were things I had no need to think about. You know, spiders and cockroaches. Lots of people are scared of bugs, so I didn't think I needed help. But ever since my job moved to a new office, I am so scared that I cannot get myself to work. I love my job to pieces, I wouldn't change it for the world, but the new building we are in was once a bakery and there are still bugs that come around looking for crumbs. I haven't seen a spider, but I have seen roaches and ants and other creepy, crawly critters. The first time it happened I actually fell to the floor. Maybe I fainted, I don't know. The next time I screamed so loudly the guys from the office upstairs came running down. I guess I'm lucky no one called 911. But, the thing is, I can't go into my office anymore. My legs just don't move me beyond the hallway. I am terrified and I get paralyzed. Can you help me? Oh, and by the way, I know that these bugs can't hurt me. I know I'm bigger than they are. Please don't insult me by asking me to be rational. I wish I could be rational about this, but my body just overtakes me."

Jen is suffering from a true phobia. She's right that it is irrational and she's right that she cannot control it. A phobia is a persistent fear that is excessive and unreasonable, and that comes into play in a specific situation. Even though the person recognizes that his or her anxiety response is extreme, he/she cannot control it.

Some therapists spend months, maybe years, trying to figure out what happened in the patient's childhood to create such an unwarranted reaction. Occasionally the therapist actually succeeds and the patient is able to identify the original cause of the fear. But, alas, that does not necessarily change the situation. Knowledge helps to understand the phobia, but rarely eradicates it.

Jen started to tell me about cruel kids in her seventh-grade class who scared her with dead ants during lunch in the school cafeteria. She wanted to tell me about her older brother, with whom she was very competitive, and she thought I'd like to know about her husband, who keeps frogs in a tank in the living room and feeds them crickets.

When I asked Jen if she had told these stories to other therapists, she replied that of course she had. But when I asked if that made any difference, the answer was no. So I said, "Let's not go there. Nothing you've done in the past has made a difference; now we'll try something new. Don't bother recounting childhood incidents; instead give me ten minutes of your time; I think I can help you."

I *was* able to help Jen. It's been about a year since she came to my office that one time, and she manages to get to work every day with no problem, no anxiety. How did I help her? I simply asked her to tap on a couple of spots on her face, a couple of spots on her hand, one spot near her neck, and another spot on her side. How long did this take? About five minutes for the entire process, including figuring out which spots would work and talking to her a little bit. She completed the actual tapping in about two minutes.

Sounds crazy, right? Many therapists won't even try the Tapping Cure. It seems too weird and too unscientific. Most psychotherapists have spent years, maybe decades, learning intricate techniques of talk therapy. A one-session method requiring almost no talk appears to be much too simplistic. One of my colleagues said, "I hope the tapping method doesn't work. I hope the results don't last. Because if they do work and they do last, then why would any patient continue coming to me for long-term treatment?" Another colleague said, "The success of tapping makes much of my previous work null and void."

WISE WORDS

Without deviation from the norm,
progress is not possible.

—Frank Zappa

SOME THEORIES

WHILE NO ONE really knows exactly how tapping works, there are many theories. Some practitioners believe that when a person goes through a difficult emotional experience, a blockage develops in his or her energy field. These people believe that energy circulates within the body, in a closed system. They believe that sometimes the energy gets stuck; it becomes blocked at a particular spot. When the energy system gets out of whack because of that blockage, a symptom will occur. Symptoms may be in the form of a phobia, as in Jen's situation, or in the form of any one of many possible emotional ailments. These practitioners believe that the person must restore balance in their now wayward energy system. They must start the energy flowing by literally thumping it into action. Of course, the thumping must be at the right spot, and it must not be serious thumping; gentle tapping is preferred.

Others believe that it is electrical activity within our nervous systems that gets mangled during an emotional situation. They claim that strong negative emotions disrupt the flow of electrical activity within the body. There are also those who believe there is a magnetic field, not an electrical field, within the body.

Is there some sort of field? If so, where, exactly, is it? Is energy really disrupted? Do thoughts disrupt the flow of energy? Do emotional reactions to a severe situation disrupt the flow of energy? Clearly, there are many theories and many theorists. Please understand that not everyone believes energy fields even exist. There is no scientific evidence, not yet, anyway, that energy is a universal life force that can influence mental health. Yet there are hundreds of practitioners who use tapping and related methods every day in their psychotherapy practices and get good results.

ENERGY PSYCHOLOGY

THE TERM *energy psychology* (EP) refers to the various techniques that combine the ideas of traditional Western psychotherapy with Eastern approaches to medicine, such as acupuncture. Holistic health practitioners who use assorted treatment modalities often define their work as part of energy psychology. Sometimes tapping is considered part of energy medicine, which may also be called vibrational medicine. Practitioners of energy psychology consider it a wonderful way to help patients without resorting to medication, but they do agree that there are many circumstances in which traditional medicine is the way to go. EP is not meant to replace conventional approaches to health care, but to supplement them or to give the patient a possible head start before beginning customary treatment. If EP works and solves the problem, then the patient need not go any further. If EP makes a difference, but does not clear up the situation in its entirety, then results from the customary treatment will be swift.

While EP may work well for the stress of anxiety or such feelings as anger or guilt or jealousy or shame, it is not the treatment of choice for symptoms or illnesses with a clearly biological cause. In that latter category are major clinical depression, bipolar disorder, schizophrenia, and most physical ailments. Some traditional doctors are against EP on principle, because they are concerned that patients will attempt to cure themselves of a disease without seeking traditional care and may, in fact, make themselves worse or miss an important diagnosis. The fear, and it is a legitimate fear, is that EP may alleviate symptoms, but not get at the underlying cause of the disease—and that then the disease might spread, making it untreatable by the time a traditional physician is consulted.

Some of the traditional physicians who are not comfortable with energy medicine will nevertheless treat a patient with ultrasound devices and Transcutaneous Electrical Nerve Stimulation (TENS) units as part of their regular protocol for pain relief. TENS therapy uses electrical stimulation to diminish pain. The TENS unit is a device that delivers low-voltage electrical current via electrodes that are placed on the skin near the source of pain. The electricity from the electrodes stimulates the nerves in an affected area. When the brain receives these electrical signals, the regular pain signals become somewhat neutralized, giving the patient some relief. EP practitioners claim this as proof that traditional doctors believe in energy fields, after all.

MERIDIANS

DR. ROGER CALLAHAN is a strong believer in energy psychology. In 1981 Dr. Callahan became a tapping pioneer when he claimed to cure psychological symptoms by simply tapping on particular points of the body. He believes that symptoms develop when energy is trapped in meridians.

What are meridians? Medical practitioners in China, and more recently some in the United States, too, believe that meridians are particular places on the skin that represent channels inside the body. A person's life force, called *Qi* or *Chi* (pronounced *chee*), is said to flow within those channels. (In India that life force is called *prana*; in secular English terms it might be fortitude and character and personality.) The life force keeps people balanced and healthy by nourishing all the cells of the body as it travels within the person. But, say the believers, that energy occasionally gets stuck or out of balance at a meridian. They believe that when Chi is properly flowing, all is right with the person; there is harmony within the body and the mind. Some people believe that each meridian is associated with a particular emotion.

Nonbelievers, of course, say that there is no meridian in human physiology and no energy or life force other than the heartbeat and pulse. Believers say that particular meridians correspond to particular internal organs. Nonbelievers say these spots are arbitrary. Many believe that Chi is a philosophical and not a scientific phenomenon.

Wise Words

The important thing is not to stop questioning.

—Albert Einstein

ANCIENT HISTORY

PERHAPS YOU'VE HEARD of Ötzi the Iceman, a man found in 1991 in the Alps on the border between Italy and Austria. He was found by hiking tourists. His body, mummified by the cold, has been carbon-dated to 3300 BC. Interestingly, he had many tattoos on his body. The tattoos were on parts of the body that we know to be acupuncture points. What does that mean? Have humans always known that they could get healing effects from certain spots on the body? Scientists from the University of Graz, in Austria, studied the

Iceman and published their findings in the prestigious medical journal *The Lancet*. They theorized that acupuncture may have been used to heal people thousands of years ago. They came to this conclusion because X-rays of Ötzi's body indicated that he suffered from arthritis of the hip, knees, ankles, and spine, and nine of the tattoos found on his body were found on spots that acupuncturists use when treating those medical conditions. The scientists concluded, "Taken together, the tattoos could be viewed as a medical report from the Stone Age, or possibly a guide for self-treatment marking where to puncture when pain occurs."

Wise Words

It is especially important to encourage unorthodox thinking when the situation is critical: at such moments every new word and fresh thought is more precious than gold. Indeed, people must not be deprived of the right to think their own thoughts.

—Boris Yeltsin

ACUPUNCTURE

TRADITIONAL CHINESE MEDICINE (TCM) endorses acupuncture as a valid approach to curing illnesses. Acupuncture is based upon the theory that the body can be healed and symptoms relieved by restoring energy balance within the body. This is done by inserting special stainless steel needles into specific meridian points. The needles are supposed to unblock the energy obstruction and thereby correct imbalances and alleviate symptoms. Sometimes low-frequency electrical current is placed on the needles to increase stimulation.

Some non-Chinese theorists of a more scientific persuasion insist that the acupuncture needles stimulate the nervous system to release chemicals that are then absorbed by the spinal cord, the brain, and muscles. Once absorbed, those chemicals reduce pain and trigger the release of other helpful substances within the body. This is based on the theory that acupuncture activates the body's natural opioid system. Opioids are brain chemicals associated with pain reduction. Some scientists believe that acupuncture alters brain chemistry by changing the release of substances in the brain that control nerve impulses. These substances are called neurotransmitters.

The National Institutes of Health (NIH) has begun several studies aimed at determining the usefulness of acupuncture. (Studies retrieved from Chinese medical journals are not considered by the medical establishment to be up to the rigorousness of American scientific standards.) Research about the efficacy of acupuncture is being conducted within a division of the NIH called the National Center for Complementary and Alternative Medicine. Thus far, they've concluded that acupuncture does some good, some of the time, for some people, under some circumstances. They believe that under certain conditions it can inhibit pain, improve circulation, and enhance immune function. They believe that in conjunction with traditional medicine acupuncture might be able to help with lower back pain, post-operative dental pain, and nausea and vomiting. The American Cancer Society endorses acupuncture as a stop-smoking technique. Even with these limited areas of approval, many folks regularly run to their acupuncturist for relief from an assortment of ailments.

MORE BODYWORK

ACUPRESSURE USES THE same points as acupuncture but does away with the needles. Instead the practitioner uses firm pressure on those spots. The spots used in tapping therapies are acupressure points.

Jin Shin Jyutsu is a Japanese form of bodywork and healing based upon the assumption that the body traps energy in particular points called energy locks. To eradicate symptoms, the energy must be freed by gently pressing on those points. This is but one alternative therapy, slowly becoming more mainstream, that uses specific points on the body to effect a significant change within the person.

There's still plenty of reluctance on the part of Western physicians to accept acupuncture and acupressure, mostly because it is not clear exactly how these techniques work. Also, traditional Western medical doctors want to know a diagnosis before they begin treating a patient, and they don't necessarily accept the premise of energy flow and its imbalances as a basis for disease or as a rationale for treatment.

THE BIRTH OF TAPPING

AS IF THE notions of acupressure and acupuncture were not sufficiently controversial, when Dr. Callahan came along in the 1980s he did not ask his patients to accept needles or to accept pressure on particular points. No, Dr. Callahan taught his clients to tap on meridian points in a specific sequence. His patients achieved some impressive results. He did not do double-blind studies. He did not do scientific clinical trials. But he did help many, many people— people who walked in with a serious symptom and left less than one hour later feeling just fine.

Roger Callahan calls his method Thought Field Therapy (TFT) and uses many tapping spots to accomplish his goal. What is a thought field? Dr. Callahan says that when we have an upsetting thought, we are actually experiencing a disruption in our body's energy system. The thought field surrounding the situation we are thinking about is, of course, invisible, but it is influencing our behavior and our feelings.

Dr. Callahan's technique has spawned many tapping teachers, each of whom adds an individual twist to further refine the procedure. Some ask their clients to speak about their problem while tapping; some ask them to think about their problem while tapping; and some prefer that their clients tap and at the same time recite affirmations indicating their acceptance of themselves. Still others demand that their clients hum and sing while tapping. Some practitioners incorporate breathing exercises into the tapping routine; others prefer that clients remain silent while tapping but concentrate on a particular mental image.

IS TAPPING UNIVERSAL?

INTERESTING, THOUGH, ISN'T it, that through the ages different cultures have advocated similar procedures to relieve distress? If there were no validity to the idea of touching particular spots on the body, would these traditions have persisted? Hazy theoretical underpinnings notwithstanding, some people must have derived some help from these methods. Chapter 2 will introduce you to all the tapping spots necessary to implement the Tapping Cure, and perhaps you, like many of my clients, will realize that you already intuitively seek out those spots on your body when you need comfort and security. Do you bite your nails when you are nervous? Certain nails are considered tapping spots. Do you rub your temples when you get upset? That area of your face is another tapping spot. As you read on, you might conclude that tapping is a natural way of self-soothing.

WISE WORDS

Tapping on the energy system while being tuned to an emotional problem is an extraordinary healing technique that is deserving of the Nobel Prize. Its impact on the healing sciences is bound to be enormous. Quite clearly, we are on the ground floor of a healing high-rise. Fortunately, there are many people experimenting with this idea and some fascinating finds are being unearthed. In time we will learn much more and will be discarding old notions for new theories.

—Gary Craig, an early adopter of tapping and the originator of a particular tapping technique

TO KNOW OR NOT TO KNOW

CHICKEN SOUP IS tasty because of the combination of vegetables and spices and broth. In order to enjoy it, we don't need to know which taste buds are stimulated, which parts of the tongue are engaged, and exactly how the food enzymes interact during digestion. To scientists, the Tapping Cure is not chicken soup. It is a procedure for changing feelings and thoughts and thus must pass more than a taste test. Scientists, rightfully, want to know how it works.

But is it necessary for my client, Jennifer, to understand why the tapping procedure worked for her? No. She is delighted, if a bit mystified, to be cured. Is it necessary for me to understand why tapping works? No, it's not necessary. Of course I would like to know the scientific foundation to this method, but not knowing has not deterred me. I am grateful to be able to help clients in one session. Even though I object to nonscientific techniques on principle, I cannot, in good conscience, ignore the evidence. And all the evidence tells me that for most people tapping works. So, I will happily continue to use this approach to healing and continue to rejoice because it has no side effects and causes no tears. My clients rejoice, too, because they quickly feel better and don't need to take out a bank loan.

I am now accomplishing in one session what used to take months and months of psychotherapy—and sometimes even after months there was no success. No harm can be caused by the tapping process; it is a benign procedure and may provide tremendous benefit. In fact, the only possible downsides to tapping are that it will have no effect (rarely) or that it will prevent you from seeking out further necessary help. So if your symptoms don't respond to tapping, please seek other professional help.

Of course, there is a downside to not knowing how or why tapping works. Due to the lack of scientific evidence, many practitioners of scientific persuasion won't even consider learning it and thus are depriving their patients of a chance of a real cure. Insurance companies refuse to pay for it. Also, thus far, not much money has been allocated to establish research studies about tapping in the United States. Without a scientific basis, there is no way to get money for government-sponsored clinical trials or randomized testing groups. Tapping may never be widely adopted in our country if it cannot be subjected to scientific scrutiny. This is what Dr. Steven Jay Lynn, professor in the Psychology Department at SUNY Binghamton, says about the science of tapping: "In the case of Thought Field Therapy, there is no reason to believe that disruptions in the body's bioenergetic system are responsible for psychological problems, and that tapping on acupoints can somehow restore psychological health. Given that there is no scientific evidence that biological currents are associated with emotional disorder, and no solid evidence that TFT reverses such currents, the treatment can be said to lack credibility. . . . Of course, it would be in the realm of possibility that another paradigm might account for what positive gains are observed following the application of TFT. However, the burden is on those who advocate TFT to both demonstrate its efficacy relative to other treatments and to provide a convincing rationale for positive outcomes associated with its application."

It is not always wrong to be skeptical of new ideas. Most fringe-science reports that seem bogus actually do turn out to be bogus. But when it is possible to observe evidence and conduct appropriate investigation, there is no excuse for rejecting a theory without examination.

True Report

LINDA SHAPIRO, A seasoned family therapist/addictions counselor, discredited the idea of tapping when I mentioned it to her several years ago. She thought it was a bogus attempt to help people who needed traditional psychotherapy. She's since changed her mind, and wrote me the following letter:

Dr. Roberta, I was desperate when I called you early that morning last week in the throes of a migraine syndrome. Despite taking prophylactic medication for chronic migraines—for which the triggers are always impossible to identify—I had awakened with a crashing headache and was in a rage, as it was the first day of a weeklong writer's workshop that I was determined to attend. But, wracked with pain, I didn't know how I would drive or whether I'd be able to concentrate even if I could get myself there. You knew I had rejected the notion of tapping years ago, yet you insisted that I give it a try. You did it over the phone, leading me through the process by telling me exactly where and how to tap and what to say while I tapped. Not only did my headache disappear, but I was headache-free throughout the day and my worrying about it disappeared, as well. I participated in my workshop, never giving a thought to the pain that had awakened me or worrying about its possible return. But then, due to the heat and humidity during the week of the workshop (or who knows why), I awakened each morning with yet another migraine. And each morning—instead of panicking—I simply tapped the headache away. I cannot thank you enough. For the moment, I don't even want to know why or how it works. I'm just enjoying its magic. Do spread the word, as only you can!

With my deepest gratitude, Linda

NO KNOWN THEORY

SOMETIMES IT IS necessary to proceed without theoretical validation. Not long ago, investment officers of a giant corporation proudly presented their year-end figures to the board of directors. Financial assets had grown to record levels, and the company's portfolio significantly outperformed the general market. One talented investment officer was responsible for the excellent results. The board members asked him to explain his investing and trading strategies. His explanation was complicated. With one exception, all members of the board agreed that the methods were amazingly successful, although difficult to comprehend. The lone dissenter was not convinced. He commented, "Yes, this works in practice, but does it work in theory?"

Tapping seems to quickly and permanently separate a particular memory from its negative feeling. After tapping, you are capable of thinking about or talking about a previously unbearable memory without having an emotional reaction. Your response will be nonchalant and neutral. Tapping eradicates the emotional pain of trauma. Also, tapping permits calmness in situations that previously caused fear or panic. You'll be able to anticipate a previously anxiety-provoking situation, such as Jen's insect phobia, and have no fear and no negativity attached to the thought. You can then go ahead and do whatever it was that used to scare you to death. Worry simply disappears.

I am here to teach you how and where to tap. You will become stress-free. Your symptoms will be gone. Presumably, one day we'll all understand how and why tapping works. Until then, there's no need for you to continue to suffer. It's time for you to get rid of your symptoms. The Tapping Cure offers you a quick and permanent cure.

Remember This

THE TAPPING CURE permits you to separate a painful emotion from a particular thought. You will be able to think about past incidents or upcoming events without negative feelings.

The Tapping Spots

Y OUR EMOTIONAL HEALTH is now in your hands—literally. Tapping will eliminate your symptoms of distress. You can get rid of negative feelings that are associated with a particular thought. You will still think your thought, but it won't be accompanied by a nasty feeling. If your painful feelings exist at all (and they probably won't), they'll seem like distant memories.

NO TALK THERAPY

No PSYCHOLOGICAL INTERACTION is necessary for the Tapping Cure to work. I don't need to hear any stories about your past—no tales of Mother, no sagas of Father, no toilet-training woes, no parenting-style issues—none of that is relevant. There is no blaming. There is no talk therapy. You are in charge. You are in control of this gentle process. There is no medicine, so there will be no side effects. You will tap yourself.

KNOW YOUR SPOTS

OUR FIRST TASK is to identify all the tapping spots on your body. Most of the spots are on your face or your hands; some are on your upper body. I will teach you all the possible spots, but don't worry; you'll probably be using only a few.

Your problem, or your obsession, or your fear, will respond to your tapping. You won't need to go to a professional. You are the expert here. You will know when tapping helps. You will learn which spots are the best spots for you to tap. It's a good idea, though, to become familiar with all the spots even if you'll be using just a small number of them. You'll soon discover that certain spots—and there's no way to predict which ones they'll be—will work better for you than others. So, knowing them all and trying them all is necessary for your success.

Results are usually evident when you tap on each appropriate spot approximately ten times, for about five seconds. Everyone is different. You may need more taps for more seconds while someone else may need fewer taps for just a couple of seconds. You might find that certain tapping spots need to be tapped more times than others.

This sounds incredible, doesn't it? In seconds your symptoms disappear. Yes, it is amazing; you will amaze yourself.

YOUR FACE

There are a number of tapping spots on your face. Let's begin with those.

Eyebrow One Spot

If you're wearing glasses, please remove them now. Touch your eyebrow—either one—it makes no difference. One tapping spot you'll be using is on the inner edge of your eyebrow, near your nose (see illustration below). Got it? This is tapping spot Eyebrow One. Using two fingers, tap on that spot. It is slightly above and to the side of your nose. Now, use your other hand to tap on that same spot. Good. Next, tap that same spot on the other eyebrow. It is the inner edge of the other eyebrow. Tap it with two fingers and then tap it with two fingers of your other hand. For tapping Eyebrow One, you now have four variations—two eyes, two hands. Try them all and decide which is most comfortable for you. Which hand seems to tap most naturally? Which eyebrow seems to feel most comfortable being tapped? Anytime you are instructed to tap Eyebrow One, you now know just how to do it.

Now, get a stopwatch or a clock and practice for about ten seconds. How many times are you tapping within those ten seconds? Now tap ten times and note how many seconds have elapsed. Usually, you'll tap each spot between five and ten seconds, between seven and twelve times. Practice now and you'll get the rhythm that works best for you. You have just perfected tapping the Eyebrow One spot. Congratulations!

Eyebrow Two Spot

We're still up on your eyebrow. Again, if you wear eyeglasses, remove them when you tap this spot. Now we're at the other edge, closest to your temple and your hairline. This is the Eyebrow Two spot. Figure out which eyebrow is easiest and most comfortable for you to tap and which hand it is most comfortable to use. Most people prefer using their dominant hand. That is, a right-handed person uses his right hand, a left-handed person, her left hand. Look at your clock and tap your Eyebrow Two spot, at the outer edge of your eyebrow, for ten seconds. Use two fingers. Good.

Under-Eye Spot

Under your eye you will feel a bony semicircle. The center of the semicircle, right under your eyeball, is called the Under-Eye spot. This spot requires three fingers for tapping, so you'll cover a wide area beneath your eye. Don't be concerned if one of your fingers is practically touching the side of your nose. That's just fine. Sometimes tapping on this spot works best when you simultaneously tap under both eyes; right hand tapping under right eye, left hand tapping under left eye. Try it now. Tap about ten times. Pause and then repeat the tapping. You may notice something interesting. For many people this is a particularly sensitive tapping spot. If you are one of these folks, you'll find that in those few seconds of tapping, your mood may have changed or perhaps a particular symptom, such as a headache, may have disappeared. But don't worry if this tapping has had no effect on you. It's not supposed to quite yet. Only those people who are extremely receptive to tapping because of some inborn biological predisposition will benefit from this little bit of under-eye tapping.

Mustache Spot

Now we'll move down your face to the spot under your nose, above your lip. This is the Mustache spot. Use four fingers to tap along the area where a moustache might grow, or maybe is growing. Use your dominant hand and tap about seven or eight times. Good.

Most people do best at this spot when they are using their dominant hand, but you are free to experiment and if you are a rightie and prefer using your left hand for tapping your Mustache spot, try it. It might work for you.

Chin Spot

This spot is directly below your lower lip. It's the spot that is probably slightly indented, the topmost part of your chin. Using four fingers, tap on the entire upper chin area. Again, there is some evidence that your dominant hand is best here, but not necessarily. Make that decision for yourself and then tap ten times. You'll be covering pretty much the entire chin area. This spot is called, aptly, the Chin spot.

Review Your Face Spots

We've now learned all the tapping spots on your face. Review them for yourself. Eyebrow One is easy to remember because it's on the side of your eyebrow closest to your nose and you have one nose. Eyebrow Two is on your eyebrow closest to your temple and you have two temples. Under-Eye, Mustache, and Chin are self-explanatory. Tap each spot a couple of times now, saying the name of the spot as you tap.

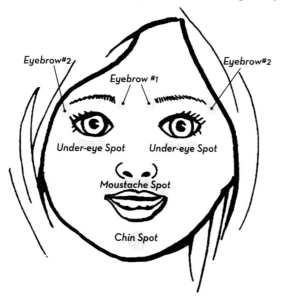

Eyebrow#2

Eyebrow #1

Eyebrow#2

Under-eye Spot

Under-eye Spot

Moustache Spot

Chin Spot

True Report

I CAN'T BELIEVE how easy it is to tap in public. No one pays attention to me when I go through all my spots. At home, at work, on the train, it makes no difference. As long as I've got my fingers attached to me, I have my best security blanket.

—Allison

YOUR HANDS

There are several tapping spots on your hands and on certain fingers. Use your dominant hand for the tapping. So, if you are left-handed, you'll be tapping on your right hand with your left; if you are right-handed, please tap on your left hand.

Karate Spot

The place on your hand that you would use when breaking a board while engaged in the practice of karate is called the Karate spot. It is the edge of your hand running from the knuckle under your pinkie until your wrist. Run your fingers along that bone to be sure you know where it is. Now tap it. You'll probably need four fingers to take in that entire area on the side of your hand.

V Spot

This spot is the "V" between your pinkie and your ring finger. Follow these instructions assuming you are right-handed. (If you are left-handed, substitute the word *right* each time you see *left* in these instructions.) Now place your left hand in front of you, on your lap or on a table, palm down. Put your right pinkie in between your left pinkie and ring finger. The other three fingers of your right hand will extend down the front of your left hand. If you wish, you may raise your left hand and do the tapping with your hand in any comfortable position. Your four fingers are extending from the V between the ring finger and the pinkie, down beyond the knuckle, heading toward the wrist. See the illustration below for a clear view of the V spot.

Pinkie Spot

This is for your littlest finger, your pinkie. Tap with one or two fingers on the spot where your nail and finger touch. While tapping, you'll actually cover the top and the sides of the nail. We're particularly interested in tapping on the side of the pinkie nail that is closest to your thumb. Got it? Good.

Index Spot

This is for your index finger. Please tap with one or two fingers on the spot where your nail and finger touch. Again, cover the entire nail and pay particular attention to the side of your nail that is closest to your thumb. While you tap, be sure to tap that side of your nail.

Thumb Spot

This is for your thumb. Tap with one or two fingers on the spot where your nail and finger touch, and be sure to include tapping on the outer edge of your thumb. (See diagram if this is confusing.)

Middle Spot

This is for your middle finger. Please tap with one or two fingers on the spot where your nail and finger touch. Again, tap on the side of the nail that is closest to your thumb.

Review Your Hand Spots

You can quickly tap on each of your finger spots—the index finger, pinkie, middle finger, and thumb. (All your fingers except the ring finger.) Then tap on your Karate spot and then your V spot. Excellent.

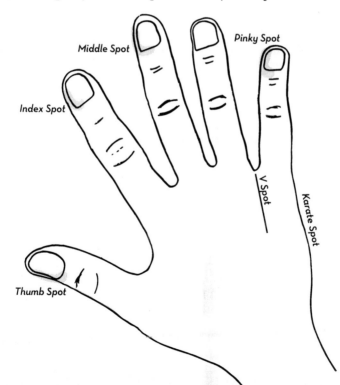

YOUR TORSO

There are several tapping spots between your neck and your waist.

Collarbone Spot

Locate the bone that travels from your shoulder straight across toward the center of your neck. You can feel the tip of the bone about one inch below your neck and then one inch to the side. Tap your collarbone using four fingers, so that one finger is at the tip of the collarbone and the other fingers are touching the bone, too. When your fingers become accustomed to tapping on this spot, you'll notice that you are actually tapping a bit below the collarbone. Many people report that they get their best results tapping a wee bit underneath, and not exactly on, the collarbone. You may use either hand to tap either collarbone. Some clients say that tapping both collarbones at once works best for them. Usually, though, it is sufficient to tap just one side. Either side, with either hand, will work just fine.

Have you ever worn a shirt that had a button-down collar? Tapping on your Collarbone is tapping at the place where a button would be if you were wearing a shirt with a button-down collar.

Side Spot

Midway between your underarm and your waist is the best spot for the tapping. If you are a woman it may be where your bra is. For a man it may be parallel to your nipple. Some people feel a soft area right at the appropriate spot. Most of us, though, have some fat covering the soft area and don't feel it. For some people the spot is a bit higher than midway and is closer to the shoulder than to the waist. It should be about four inches below your underarm. Tap your side using four fingers. Most people find it easiest to use the right hand to tap on the left side, or the left hand to tap on the right side, but you may do it any way that is comfortable for you. Some people use the hand on the same side of their body and tap using their thumb.

Pledge Spot

This is a spot on the left side of your chest and it is a spot that is not tapped; instead it is rubbed, gently, with your knuckles. It's a couple of inches below your left shoulder and a couple of inches in from your left side, going toward the center of your chest. You can easily find this spot if you put your right hand in position to pledge allegiance to the flag. While your hand is on your chest in that position, make a fist. Your knuckles are now on the Pledge spot. Simply move your fist in a circle, lightly pressing your knuckles on that spot. Go around and around a couple of times. Practice now.

These are the only spots you'll need to know. You are a unique individual and your body chemistry is unique, too. Thus, certain spots that will work well for you may not work well for your friend. That is OK. There are many alternate possibilities in this tapping cure.

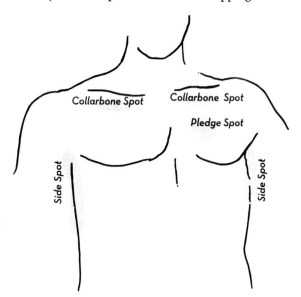

EVERYDAY TAPPING SPOTS?

IS THERE ANYTHING familiar to you about these tapping spots? Do they seem to be parts of your body that you sometimes touch? Think about what you do when you are upset. You probably have your own self-soothing rituals that you do without even realizing it. For example, do you bite your nails? Do you chew your cuticles? Some people, when they become frightened or nervous, feel compelled to bite and chew particular areas of their fingers. Interestingly, usually those are particular tapping spots. You might intuitively have known that putting pressure on certain fingers gives comfort.

If you are not a nail biter, might you be a ring twirler? A knuckle clencher? Or maybe you are a hand wringer? I've observed people in distress squeeze one hand with the other, and then reverse it and have the second hand squeeze the first. All of these finger and hand maneuvers usually correspond to the very spots described here as curative spots.

I have some friends who, when they feel stressed, run to the nearest nail salon. Is it because their nail polish is chipping? Is it because a nail has broken? Or might it be that they love getting a manicure because during the manicure process their fingers and hands are touched, prodded, and, yes, tapped? Spa centers are popping up all over and they often offer manicures as part of their stress-relief program. So, perhaps tapping is not all that unusual, after all.

Consider what you do when you meet someone and want to demonstrate that you accept and welcome them—you shake their hand! Folklorists tell us that in ancient times when a villager met a stranger, each would cautiously reach for his dagger and they would circle one another. Once they were assured that they were not enemies out to kill, they'd return the daggers to their sheaths and extend their empty hands to one another. This was a sign of friendship. Once they touched hands, and perhaps even inadvertently tapped, they grew confident that they were safe.

Next time you shake someone's hand, notice which parts of the hand are being gripped. Certainly you've touched, and maybe even tapped, the Karate spot. This is yet more evidence that the Tapping Cure may not be that unusual; it may simply be a formalized way of accomplishing what we all intuitively know—that touching certain areas on hands and fingers makes us, and others, feel better.

Throughout the centuries, in every part of the world, women, and often men, too, have adorned their fingers. Look at your hands now. Are you wearing a ring? More than one ring? What does that ring mean to you? Does it give you comfort? Would it give you the same feeling of comfort if it were on your toe? Probably not. There is something important, maybe even necessary, about touching your fingers.

Are you wearing other jewelry? Is there a gold chain circling your neck? A strand of pearls? Is a religious symbol hanging from your neck jewelry? And when you move, when you walk, is your neck jewelry tapping your collarbone? When you are upset, do you self-soothe by touching your neck jewelry and perhaps moving it right onto that collarbone area? Through the ages, humans have placed adornment in places near or on the spots that have been identified as part of the Tapping Cure.

Hot Spots

A quick anti-stress cure is to say what it is that is bothering you while rubbing your Pledge spot with your knuckles. End your sentence by adding . . . *I'm OK.*

What do *you* do when you want to make yourself feel better? Do you hug yourself, putting your arms across your chest and placing each hand directly on your side tapping spots? Do you actually tap? Pay attention the next time you hug yourself. Many people automatically move their fingertips up and down while in that self-hugging position.

Similarly, most of us have, at some point, hugged someone in an effort to ease their pain. Did you tap your fingers on their side while embracing? If so, you were tapping on the Side spots.

What do you do when you are thinking about a problem and want to clear your mind? Do you place your chin in the palm of your hand and extend your fingers up your face? If you do, then you are among the many people who unconsciously tap under their eyes when they wish to feel better. Try that position now and notice if it feels familiar. Notice that once your fingers are in that area under your eye, they will automatically begin tapping.

Maybe you're one of those folks who does not put their chin in one hand but in both hands. If you do that it's likely that instead of tapping under your eyes, you'll be tapping both temples. Or maybe you'll be rubbing your temples. Some people rub their temples whenever they want to relax. Do you?

RELIGION AND TAPPING SPOTS

WHEN A CATHOLIC person makes the sign of the cross, particular finger configurations are made and particular body parts—forehead, chest, and shoulders—are touched. When an Orthodox Jewish man uses tefillin as part of his daily prayer ritual, he is putting pressure on particular points of his hands, arms, and face. No matter your culture or your religion, chances are there is a ceremony that entails pressing or tapping some of the spots used in the Tapping Cure.

It's possible that you've been using the Tapping Cure for years without even knowing it. You might have been stimulating your healing spots unconsciously. The difference between what you may have been doing to self-soothe and what you will now do is that this formalized method is more extensive and will give you a permanent cure, not a temporary fix.

BORN LUCKY?

CERTAIN SPOTS WILL immediately eliminate certain symptoms. Some people respond with great favor to tapping on one or two spots. When they tap on those spots, their symptoms vanish, their anxiety disappears, and their phobia is gone.

Are you one of those lucky folks? Let's find out. Choose one issue you'd like to change in your life. Perhaps you want to get rid of your memory of a childhood schoolyard fight that still haunts you. Or maybe it's your fear of presenting a sales presentation to a new prospect. Or, could it be the nervousness you feel when you meet someone new, or the embarrassment you still experience when you think about something silly you said in front of your neighbors?

Hot Spots

Feeling worried or tense? For quick relief, try tapping on your Under-Eye spot and your Collarbone spot. Tap:

Under-Eye, Collarbone, Under-Eye, Collarbone.

REPORT CARD

THIS IS AN initial practice, just for fun. Think about the incident that is bothering you. Let's say you are nervous about an upcoming meeting with your supervisor. Now, imagine a report card that uses a grading system of A, B, C, D, and F. F represents the worst possible feeling you could have about that meeting. You are certain you'll be humiliated and then perhaps demoted or even fired. You are certain you'll say and do the absolute wrong thing. When your report card shows an F, you know that you are so miserable you can barely tolerate your emotions. F represents the most severe emotion you experience when you think about your situation.

D means you are pretty upset, but your feelings are somewhat tolerable. You anticipate a difficult meeting with your supervisor, but you can get through it.

C is better than D, but still not good. You are nervous and cannot eat, but otherwise you're OK.

B means that although the situation still bothers you, you are not terribly upset. You know that soon this meeting will be done with and you'll get through it without too much trouble.

A represents a perfect peaceful feeling. Nothing bothers you when your report card indicates you are at A. You are looking forward to the meeting with your supervisor. You want to strut your stuff. You want to talk about your accomplishments and your ideas for the future.

Before you begin tapping, think about the situation that is causing you a problem and give your upset feelings a rating. Decide if your feelings, when you think of the situation, are at an A, B, C, D, or F.

QUICK FIX

NEXT, THINK ABOUT the situation and start to tap. Remember, this is just a trial run to prepare you for the actual tapping we'll soon do. This is to see if your body might respond to tapping in a robust way—in a way that produces immediate results. You never know, you might have been born with the ability to cure yourself quickly and easily. Your body and your mind might respond promptly to tapping.

Think about your situation, think about how upset you are, and choose a tapping spot, any spot, and start tapping. Tap for about five to seven seconds. That's all you need to do.

After tapping, take a deep breath and relax for a moment. Now think about your issue once again. Is it still as disturbing as it was? What letter represents it now? Try another spot and repeat the tapping while thinking of your situation. Approximately half the clients who come to my office obtain immediate relief just by tapping on one of these spots. The most usual spots for quick help from tapping are Under-Eye and Collarbone.

Just tap on either one of these spots, or you might try both of them. You might do Under-Eye, then Collarbone, then Under-Eye, and then Collarbone again. If you are a quick responder, this will immediately provide relief. If you have no response, then you are like the rest of us and will need to go more deeply into this technique — and we'll do that right away. But if you do get partial relief, please continue tapping for a few minutes and you may very well clear up your entire problem in record time.

Visualize your report card. Think about the upsetting incident or situation. What letter now pops up on your report card? Are you getting better? If you are, continue with the tapping until you are totally an A. If you already are an A, then you know you've cured yourself. Congratulations.

For a permanent cure, you'll tap in a more formalized way and you will accompany your tapping strokes with words. It is those words, along with the appropriate tapping spots, that will heal you. Now that you know all about where to tap, I'll teach you what to say while you tap.

Remember This

IT IS NOT necessary for you to do any memorizing. Simply follow the illustrations to know where to tap. It's OK to tap any spots, in any sequence. You will figure out your best tapping spots after a while.

Here is a list to remind you of all the tapping spots. When you are instructed to tap a full sequence, you will be using all of these spots.

Eyebrow One	Pinkie
Eyebrow Two	Index
Under-Eye	Thumb
Mustache	Middle
Chin	Collarbone
Karate	Side
V	Pledge

Talking and Tapping

WHILE YOUR FINGERS tap, your mind needs to be busy, too. Your mind needs to be thinking terrible thoughts. Yes, that's right. Even though people usually tell you to cheer up and think positive, I am instructing you to feel very upset. It is necessary for you to summon up your negative emotions while you tap. In order for your painful feelings to be worked on by your tapping, those painful feelings must be foremost in your mind.

Please, make yourself miserable. You will get your best results when you are feeling bad. Allow your imagination to run wild. The more upset you become during this brief exercise, the more successful you'll be at curing yourself.

It is necessary to clearly identify your situation. If it is a memory that is troubling you, try to relive it in your mind. If it is a thought or worry, see it and confront it in your mind. As you think about these upsetting circumstances, give yourself permission to feel the negative feelings. Allow yourself to feel your raging emotions. Make yourself feel worse. Let your emotions torture you.

True Report

I'M NOT ONE for therapy, but I was willing to try Dr. Roberta's method because it wouldn't break the bank and because it didn't seem like real therapy. I had to find a way to get over the hurt about my mother not wanting to come to my wedding. The doc had me do this tapping stuff, but first she told me to think about how sad I felt. I actually cried and then I got angry at my mother. But all those feelings disappeared once I started the tapping. In just a few minutes my emotions were calmer than ever and they've stayed that way.

—Adam

Don't worry. This is a brief procedure, and in a few minutes all the negative feelings that you are brave enough to face will be gone. Not only will they be gone for the moment, they will be gone forever. The severest negative state you can experience will become your quickest route to recovery. You will soon have no negative emotion associated with this particular thought. You will successfully reach your goal, which is to separate your horrifying feeling from a particular memory or particular thought.

The Tapping Cure is swift, effective, and easy to do. The only complicated part of the treatment is figuring out precisely what you are tapping for. Sometimes, like Adam, you might think you are sad, but under the sadness lies anger. So, like Adam, you would need to tap for both sadness and anger. It's possible to tap for one part of a situation and still have a huge component of that problem unaddressed, and thus not tapped for. But talking about the situation usually brings out all the hidden feelings. For example, sometimes what originally seems like grief could, in fact, be loneliness; what seems like anger might actually be frustration. Many situations have several angles to them. I'll teach you how to formulate several sentences or phrases to help you in complex situations. Each of the angles in your situation will require tapping. For now, though, let's begin with a simpler situation—a situation that needs but one thought about which you'll tap.

Once you know the specific upsetting situation you want to address, you can reduce it to one phrase or sentence. Don't rush; forming an accurate sentence is a challenge that may take a few minutes to figure out.

Let's get started. Your sentence, or phrase, must be specific. It should describe the particular incident or circumstance, memory or obsession that is causing you pain. Some useful examples:

- *I still remember when I was mugged.*
- *My girlfriend wants to leave me.*
- *I can't believe my brother didn't choose me for his best man.*

Remember, your sentence has to do with you. You have the ability to make changes in *your* life, but you do not have the ability to change other people. Nor do you have the ability to change certain immutable facts. Please do not construct a sentence reflecting your desire to grow four inches, to have blue eyes, to cure your disease, to make your love interest marry you, or to get your neighbor to treat you more respectfully or your boss to give you a raise. In the examples above, tapping will help the client get over the feelings associated with his girlfriend leaving him, but it will not force her to remain with him. Similarly, the man whose brother chose someone else to be the best man at his wedding will master his feelings, but he will not change his brother's choice.

I took some notes during my most recent sessions and jotted down the most effective sentences that we used for my clients' specific problems. Here is a list that demonstrates some of the issues for which tapping is useful and also demonstrates the best type of sentence/phrase construction.

TYPICAL TAPPING SENTENCES

- I get enraged when I think of how my father criticized me every day
- I am scared of water and afraid to go sailing with my husband
- I can't stand myself when I make a mistake
- My wife never listens to me and I'm going crazy from the way she handles our kids
- My mother never loved me and I am so hurt
- I hate myself because I'm too fat
- I'm all alone in the world and always feel lonely
- I hurt my son and I can't forgive myself

True Report

MY MOTHER DIED when I was young. I never knew my father. I am an only child and I have no knack for making friends. I guess I'm just a loser. I'm the only one on the planet who goes to McDonald's on Thanksgiving—and forget about Christmas. I just stay in bed. I don't know where to begin, there's so much wrong with me and my life. Basically, I'm by myself from the minute I get home from work until the next day at the office. Tapping can't get me a mother or a father or a sister or a brother, so what can it do? Probably nothing.

OK, so I tried it. Dr. Roberta told me just to focus on my loneliness and I did. Then she told me what to say and where to tap. And for some reason, I don't really know why, I've been sleeping through the night without nightmares and I've been thinking that maybe I'm not so bad after all. I'm even considering talking to my next-door neighbor about going out for a drink one night next week. I haven't done it yet, but it doesn't seem too difficult. I can't believe this is all from tapping, so maybe it's not. But tapping is the only new thing I've done in my life.

—Annabelle

It was not easy for my clients to come up with their sentences. They each had long stories to tell. Each story finally was reduced to one phrase or sentence. Here are two typical stories and the ways in which we whittled them down to one sentence.

Nanette: *I was on the bus and the bus driver was nasty. He actually yelled at me to step to the rear and I did. I am an obedient person. I was raised to listen to authority. But from the back of the bus I could see that other passengers were standing in the front, right where I had been. The driver didn't say anything to them. I got so mad. Why was he picking on me? That day I couldn't concentrate on my work. My boss was out so it didn't matter too much, but now it's a week later and I still can't pay attention to anything. I keep thinking about the nerve of that guy. How dare he criticize me and tell me what to do. And I guess that's why I'm here now. I don't take suggestions too well. Anytime anyone tries to give me advice I think they are attacking me. Sometimes they are, but other times they're just being helpful. Their helpfulness gets me mad—really, really angry. Why don't they just leave me alone?*

Dr. Roberta: *So, these feelings didn't originate on the bus; you've had them before?*

Nanette: *Oh, yes. My dad was relentless. He had something to say about everything I did. Nothing I did was right. It always had to be his way. We had fights every day. And no matter how angry I was, I had to shove it and be respectful.*

Dr. Roberta: *Does this continue to this day?*

Nanette: *No, my father passed away six years ago. But I still become enraged whenever people butt in to my life. I get fired from jobs more than most other office managers. In fact, I don't know of any office managers who've ever lost their jobs. And me, I go through a few jobs and a couple of bosses every year.*

Dr. Roberta: *So, what is it you want to accomplish here today?*

Nanette: *I want to take it in stride when someone gives me advice or direction. I don't want to react with fury.*

Dr. Roberta: *If you were able to stop thinking of the way in which your father treated you, would you be able to be more tolerant of advice-givers?*

Nanette: *Yes, but I can never get my father out of my mind. Not a day goes by when I don't hear him yelling at me for something or other.*

And then Nanette and I formulated her sentence: *I get enraged when I think of how my father criticized me every day.*

This worked well for Nanette as a basic sentence and soon she accomplished what she'd come for.

Lila: *Please help me. I am so miserable. My husband and I sold our house and moved to a new community. Our house is the most beautiful home I've ever seen. But now that we're retired, my husband has the time and the money to pursue his dream—to become a Sunday sailor. We bought a boat and he is in heaven. Our community is a boating community and every house has a dock out back. I was never into water. I grew up not knowing how to swim. In fact I almost didn't graduate from college because I couldn't pass the Red Cross test. Well, my fear of water still exists. Oh, I'm fine inside our gorgeous new home. But I hate to go out back. To me, the boat looks like it's about to collapse into the water. And now my husband is annoyed with me. I keep making excuses about why I cannot accompany him, but he probably knows the truth. You will never get me on that boat or on any boat. I need to stay on land. He goes out without me, but he looks so sad. I have disappointed him. He wanted us to spend these years sailing up and down the coast. While he was planning the boating adventures I thought I'd be able to overcome my fears. It all seemed like the distant future. But it's here now and I can't overcome my fears. Sometimes I think I should tell him to divorce me. He's worked hard for so many years and now I am preventing him from enjoying himself.*

Dr. Roberta: *So what exactly do you want to accomplish here today?*

Lila: *I need some counseling, I guess. Maybe you could give me advice. Should I suggest a divorce to my husband? Or should I go back to work and have a good excuse not to join him? Or do you think I should make him give up the boat? It tortures me to see him so sad when I don't go with him. I am miserable these days. I've been a good wife and I've never made him unhappy before. What should I do?*

Dr. Roberta: *Lila, the bad news is that you've got a true phobia. The good news is that I know a way for you to get rid of your phobia—today. It's not hard to do with tapping. In fact, you'll probably leave here today ready to walk on your dock and hop on the boat.*

Lila: *It's not possible for me to get rid of my water fears. I've tried for years and nothing works.*

I then explained that our next step would be to construct a sentence. Lila suggested a few:

- *I want my husband to be happy and not angry with me.*
- *I want to find a way to sell our house and move back inland.*
- *I want to become motivated to go back to work and be busy every day.*

Of course none of these suggestions is suitable. The first is not possible to accomplish because there is no way to control another person's feelings. If her husband feels unhappy or angry he will remain so until he, himself, decides to do something about it.

The second and third sentences are predicated on the premise that Lila will always have her water phobia. If she enjoyed the water, she would prefer sitting on her boat with her husband to sitting in an office cubicle. And, of all the places they've ever lived, Lila confessed that this house is the one she loves the most.

I suggested that her water phobia is what is causing her anguish, and that is what she should address in her tapping. She chose her basic sentence to be: *I am scared of water and afraid to go sailing with my husband.*

A few weeks after our session Lila just happened to notice an ad in the local newspaper about private swim lessons for adults. She called, she went, and now she swims and she accompanies her husband on boating weekends.

YOUR TURN

NOW YOU WILL learn to construct your sentence and then expand it. First, identify the feeling you want to get rid of. Is it:

- Rage?
- Fear?
- Shame?
- Anger?
- Panic?
- Hatred?
- Guilt?
- Frustration?
- ????

Next, identify the memory or thought or behavior that is disturbing you. From the above list, here are examples of painful memories:

- Memory of father's criticisms
- Memory of mother's lack of love
- Memory of harming son

From the above list, here are examples of painful thoughts of the future:

- Fear of water
- Fear of making a mistake

From the above list, here are examples of painful current thoughts:

- Upset about wife's actions
- Hatred of appearance
- Lonely because no family

Construct your sentence—or it might be just a phrase—using your thought or memory, and your feeling. Describe your dilemma as best you can in just a few words. Now, write down your words.

REPORT CARD TIME

REMEMBER THE GRADING system with letters A through F that we used in chapter 2? It's time for you to grade your feelings now. When you think about your situation, how upset are you? Remember that to achieve your goal of A, perfectly at peace with this situation, you'll need to start out at D or F. F is the worst possible feeling; D is pretty bad but tolerable. How upset are you when you read those words you wrote? Please activate your strong emotions. Rate your distress and try to get your level up as high as possible. When you are ready, please write down your letter grade.

The more you arouse your negative feelings, the more rapidly they will disappear after tapping. When a memory is reactivated, with all its negative emotions, and when a thought is reflected upon, with all its negative emotions, a particular process occurs in your brain. Your brain permits your perception of the incident to become pliable and malleable. This is called neural plasticity. This is the moment when an appropriate intervention can change the emotional memory. This is when tapping can dissipate the emotions. This is when you can go from an F to an A.

NEXT STEP

YOUR SENTENCE IS written and your letter grade is recorded. Now take a moment to read your statement. Say it out loud. Good. Now you will make a slight addition to your wording. You will add a few words before and after your sentence.

The words to appear **before** are: *Even though*

The words to appear **after** are: *I am OK*

In the examples taken from my clients, their sentences now read:

- *Even though* I get enraged when I think of how my father criticized me every day, *I am OK.*
- *Even though* I am scared of water and afraid to go sailing with my husband, *I am OK.*
- *Even though* I can't stand myself when I make a mistake, *I am OK.*
- *Even though* my wife never listens to me and I'm going crazy from the way she handles our kids, *I am OK.*
- *Even though* my mother never loved me and I am so hurt, *I am OK.*
- *Even though* I hate myself because I'm too fat, *I am OK.*
- *Even though* I'm all alone in the world and always feel lonely, *I am OK.*
- *Even though* I hurt my son and I can't forgive myself, *I am OK.*

KEY WORDS

IN ADDITION TO your report card letter grade, you now have one sentence written on your piece of paper. It begins with *Even though* and it ends with *I am OK*. Please read your sentence aloud. Good. Next, I'd like you to think of a key word—a word that will represent this entire sentence to you. That way you won't always have to read the entire sentence; you'll sometimes just say the key word, and hearing that word will bring your sentence into your mind.

Here are key words for the examples listed above:

- *Even though* I get enraged when I think of how my father criticized me every day, *I am OK*. Key word: **criticism**
- *Even though* I am scared of water and afraid to go sailing with my husband, *I am OK*. Key word: **water**
- *Even though* I can't stand myself when I make a mistake, *I am OK*. Key word: **perfection**
- *Even though* my wife never listens to me and I'm going crazy from the way she handles our kids, *I am OK*. Key word: **wife**
- *Even though* my mother never loved me and I am so hurt, *I am OK*. Key word: **mother**
- *Even though* I hate myself because I'm too fat, *I am OK*. Key word: **fat**
- *Even though* I'm all alone in the world and always feel lonely, *I am OK*. Key word: **loneliness**
- *Even though* I hurt my son and I can't forgive myself, *I am OK*. Key word: **son**

Write your key word right underneath your sentence. You are now ready to begin tapping and to cure yourself. Let's go!

ᴄ⎰ɪꜱᴇ ᴄ⎰ᴏʀᴅꜱ

Uttering a word is like striking a note on the key-board of the imagination.

—Ludwig Wittgenstein

LET THE TAPPING BEGIN

PLEASE CONSULT THE chart on page 189 to guide you through your tapping spots.

KARATE SPOT

Remind yourself where your Karate spot is. Using four fingers, tap on your Karate spot. While tapping, please read your sentence two times. Just tap. Nothing fancy. No hard banging on the side of your hand. Don't hurt yourself. Tap while you read the sentence twice. Say your sentence clearly; say it loudly; shout it out. Say it with conviction—even if you have none. Say it with sincerity—even if you don't mean it. While you are saying it, please think about your suffering. Remember how much pain you are feeling and allow yourself to feel it more and more.

PLEDGE SPOT

Now remind yourself where the Pledge spot is. Remember, this spot is not tapped, it is rubbed. Rub your Pledge spot in a circle, while once again saying aloud your full sentence. Even if you don't believe the sentence, act as if you do and say it clearly. Good job!

KEY WORD ONLY

It's time to revert to the key word. For the next tapping sequences, you will simply say your key word while thinking about your distress. You will begin with the tapping spots on your face and work your way down to your hands and to your torso. Refer to the tapping chart on pages 192–193 to guide you.

Throughout your tapping, your aim is to bring out your negative feelings so that you can eradicate them. Work your way through the tapping spots listed on the chart, saying your key word with the taps.

With each new spot feel how upset you are—feel your fear, or anger, or hatred, or discomfort.

Say your key word, focus on your situation, feel miserable, and begin tapping on Eyebrow One. Suffer! After about five seconds, or about seven to ten taps, move on to Eyebrow Two. Do the same on Eyebrow Two and then proceed to Under-Eye, and then Mustache and Chin.

Pause and take a deep breath, and then proceed to your hand. Saying the key word and focusing on your situation, allow yourself to feel very upset as you tap your V spot, and then Pinkie, Index, Thumb, and Middle spots.

Again, pause and take a deep breath, and then go to your Collarbone spot and your Side spot. Say your key word and think about your situation as you tap on each spot. Good.

Now that you have completed all your spots, please tap on your Karate spot once again and this time say your complete sentence, not just the key word. Say your sentence two times while you tap and bring your problem to mind.

REPORT CARD TIME

PAUSE AND CLOSE your eyes while thinking about your situation. See what letter pops up on your report card. Is it still an F? Is it a D? Are you feeling better? Are you at C? B? Did you cure yourself—are you at A?

If you've gone down a letter or two, it's time to do the tapping once again. Begin with your Karate spot, then rub your Pledge spot. Now go on to the tapping spots on your face and then on your hand. Next go to Collarbone spot and Side spot, then finish with the Karate spot once again.

You may have noticed that although this may sound complicated, going through the entire sequence beginning and ending with the Karate spot takes about two minutes.

BEST SPOTS

RATE YOUR LEVEL of upset once again. If you are continuing to go down, one letter at a time, then just keep tapping until you are at an A. You may notice that certain spots are better than others. You may notice that whenever you tap under your eye, you feel a sense of relief. Or, perhaps for you it is the Mustache spot that gives you extra comfort. Experiment with omitting those tapping spots that don't seem to do much for you. Some people need just two or three spots. Others need all the hand and finger spots but only one on their face. Most everyone benefits from the Collarbone spot. One client of mine needed only the Side spot to totally recover from a lifelong phobia. But she needed to use the Karate spot, too, as an ending spot. So take the time to figure out your best spots and concentrate on tapping them. You can't go wrong by tapping all the spots and thus doing a full sequence.

Please remember that psychiatrists know that the antidepressant that works for Jill may have no effect upon Jack; internists know that the antibiotic that cures Hannah may not reduce Harry's fever at all. So, too, your tapping spots are unique to you. Take the time to figure out your best spots and perhaps your best sequence, too. Most people respond well to the Karate spot as a first and last tapping spot. Do you?

YOUR GOAL

YOUR REPORT CARD will have an A—that is your goal. When you can think of your original situation—the trauma or memory or fear—that so distressed you without feeling any of that distress, then you know you can accurately say you are at an A. When my clients tell me that they are down to an A after tapping, I ask them to visualize their upsetting situation and tell me if they agree with these statements:

- It's no big deal
- I can handle that
- It no longer disturbs me
- That's in my past; I don't really care about it today
- I accept myself; I am just fine

When they say that they agree with these statements, I know they have received the Tapping Cure. Now it is your turn to receive the Tapping Cure. Tap yourself until you, too, can agree with the five statements above. Perhaps you can add a few more statements, too.

STUCK?

OCCASIONALLY A CLIENT will move from an F to a B, but get stuck at B. If you get to an A, then you have a good chance of being cured for life, so I don't want my clients, or you, to settle for a B. Sometimes you need only tap through all your spots a few more times. But sometimes you might need to slightly change your original sentence and then tap through the sequence again, this time saying your full new sentence.

If you've gone through your tapping spots several times and you're still stuck at a B, it's time to make a change in your sentence.

The change in the sentence is as follows: instead of adding *I am OK* to the end of the sentence, we change it to *I will soon be OK*. For some unknown reason it seems that certain people need to get rid of their pain slowly, and their mind won't let them feel totally fine all at once. If this is your situation, then once you replace *I am OK* with *I will soon be OK*, you'll see a difference in how you feel. You will then need to tap later on in the day and a couple of times the next day to finally reach your goal.

Your goal is to dissolve your painful emotions, but still have access to your original thought or memory. When you reach A you will have replaced your anguish with calm and your fear with neutrality. You will actually be able to visualize a new way of experiencing your thought.

NO SUCCESS?

ARE YOU STILL upset? Are you still at an F? Don't worry. It's not your fault. You were tapping just fine. Usually, the problem is that your sentence is not the right sentence. No need to be concerned; we can fix that. Emotional situations are tricky and complex. Sometimes there's more to a situation than is at first apparent.

LORRAINE

LET ME TELL you about Lorraine. Lorraine made an appointment, sobbing on the phone. She was extremely distraught and had actually broken out in a case of hives, which her doctor attributed to "high anxiety." What was making Lorraine so anxious? Her son's wedding.

"Well," I said, "every mom gets a bit excited when a child's wedding is coming up."

"Oh, no," said Lorraine, "this is not an ordinary situation. This is going to be the very first time I will see my ex-husband since our divorce eight years ago."

I innocently thought that was the whole story, and we tapped for the sentence: *Even though I will see my ex-husband I am OK.*

Lorraine did not budge from her F grade.

We talked some more, and Lorraine revealed that her husband had left her for another woman and that that woman, the new wife, was going to be at the wedding, too.

Now we tapped for: *Even though I will be in the same room as the slut I am OK.*

Lorraine tapped and went from F to D but could get no further after many attempts.

We talked more. Now Lorraine revealed that she was embarrassed to be seen by her ex-husband and his new wife. In the years since the divorce, Lorraine had put on weight, become gray-haired, and stopped caring about her clothes. She looked her age, which was in her fifties. Trouble was, the new wife was thirty-two and Lorraine anticipated feeling old and looking haggard when standing near her. This time we tapped to: *Even though I look old enough to be the mother of the groom I am OK.* This sentence served two purposes. It reflected the true situation of Lorraine's discomfort, and also reinforced her position of honor at the wedding.

Lorraine tapped three full sequences, moving from D to B to A. She left my office an hour and a half after arriving. (This was a long session. Usually tapping sessions last less than one hour.) As she was leaving, Lorraine looked back at me and said, "Why would I care if the idiot and his wife are at the wedding. It's my day to shine."

Two weeks later Lorraine called. The wedding was a success. She was a success. Her hives were gone. And she looked forward to visiting the newlyweds in their home just down the street from her ex. "If I bump into him or his wife, why, that'll be their problem," she said.

Lorraine's words on the phone to me demonstrated true success. True success is feeling that the original situation that was so frightening or difficult is now "no big deal."

ᗯise ᗯords

All truths are easy to understand once they are discovered; the point is to discover them.

—Galileo

ANGLES

Lorraine's story illustrates the need to look at your situation from different angles if the tapping does not work on your first go-around. Sometimes you don't realize that there are other aspects to a situation that need to be addressed. Sometimes after clearing up one aspect, another emerges. That's fine; you can clear up the next and the next, too. It only takes a couple of minutes to do the tapping for each issue.

CHECK-UP TIME

CHECK TO BE sure you've figured out the right phrase, figured out which angles are important, and figured out which tapping spots are best for you, and you should be on your way to success.

If you've done your best, tried many angles, and yet are still suffering, it's time to look beyond tapping. Please seek out a mental health professional and state your case. There is hope for you. You can feel better.

Now that you know how to tap—where to drum your fingers and what to say while doing so—let's learn how to tap away fears. Phobias respond well to the Tapping Cure.

Remember This

HERE'S HOW YOU rate your situation: If you are not upset at all, then your grade is an A. But if you are distressed, represent your negative feelings with one of the following letter grades.

B = not perfect, but almost
C = somewhat upset
D = very upset
F = unbearably upset

Fears
and Phobias

EVERYONE IS SCARED of something. But not everyone is so frightened that their fear prohibits them from functioning. When Andrew came to my office, he admitted that he had sat in his car, in my driveway, for about fifteen minutes just to be sure. What did he need to be sure of? Andrew needed to be sure that there were no dogs nearby. He checked the driveway. He checked the sidewalk. He checked the bushes and the hedges. Only when Andrew was certain that there were no dogs waiting to pounce on him did he feel brave enough to leave the car—and then he ran like crazy to quickly duck into the entrance.

A FEAR OF DOGS

ANDREW KNOWS THAT his fear of dogs is irrational. He is not irrationally afraid of anything else, yet he is extremely afraid of dogs. This is a true phobia. A phobia is an excessive fear of a specific thing. It is a fear that is totally out of proportion to the actual possible danger. The only way that the phobic person can relieve the intense symptoms of terror is to avoid the frightening object.

Most people who have a phobia are perfectly normal and healthy. Usually, they are not afraid of anything other than their one feared object. Do you have a phobia? If you are terribly afraid of something, but you can avoid coming into contact with it and can conduct your life with ease while avoiding it, you don't have a phobia. You simply have a fear. Fears become phobias when they interfere with your daily functioning.

Andrew reported that he rarely ventured out of his house and that he never finished college because the phobia began while he was a college student. He had to take a leave of absence from school and simply stay at home with his parents. Rationally, he knew that there were no dogs living on campus. But, he thought, what if a faculty member brings in a dog from home or what if a stray dog wanders onto the campus? Now it is years later and he is still home with his parents. As luck would have it, Andrew worked from his computer so he never needed to venture out to earn a living.

There are many theories about how and why phobias develop, but for most people there is no true answer. Sometimes a frightening experience catalyzes the phobia, but often there is no such experience at all. Andrew remembers being in a chemistry class and overhearing a conversation between two of his lab partners. One of them had been bitten by a dog over the weekend. Andrew said nothing, but began to think that dogs would attack him after class, on his way back to his dorm. He remained in his dorm room for the next several days. His roommate brought him food from the dining hall.

By the end of that week he called his parents to come and get him. He knew that something bizarre was going on. His parents tried to reason with him, but Andrew's phobia, like anyone else's phobia, was not responsive to reason. Andrew's parents tried to get him to overcome his extreme fear. They consulted many professionals and were told that the usual method of treating phobias is a system of gradually introducing the feared object back into the person's life. This is called *systematic desensitization*. The phobic person is trained, in stages, to be less sensitive to the feared object.

For Andrew that meant that for the first few days his mom would borrow a neighbor's dog, put it on a leash, and walk by the living room window while Andrew looked out. After a few days he presumably would be able to tolerate looking at the dog, and then his mom would bring it closer to the window. Eventually it would be brought into the living room on a leash. Over time—days, weeks, maybe months—Andrew would be able to be in the same room as the leashed dog. The dog then would be unleashed but securely held in Mom's lap. Next, the dog and Mom would sit next to Andrew. Eventually Andrew should be able to pet the dog while it is in Mom's lap. From there, progress would be made and—well, you get the point. But, alas, none of this ever happened. Andrew could not tolerate looking out the window at the dog. He became so panic-stricken and so frightened that the plan could not proceed. His parents were desperate. He was desperate. So desperate were they that they agreed to make an appointment with me after a neighbor told them about my strange, but effective, Tapping Cure. And that's how Andrew made his way to my office one day last spring.

Andrew: *Hello, Doctor. I feel like an idiot. You can't imagine how my heart is racing and how close I felt to death trying to run here. This is the first time I've been out in the open since this all began. Do you want to hear about the day it began?*

Dr. Roberta: *No, Andrew, that won't be necessary. I understand that this phobia is a nasty intruder in your life and I want to get rid of it swiftly.*

Andrew: *How many sessions will I need? I don't think I could go through this again. It was really painful to get into here.*

Dr. Roberta: *We are going to cure you today. In a few minutes you'll know just what to do and you will do it and you will get the phobia out of you. Let's begin.*

Andrew: *I don't think I'll be able to do anything worthwhile now. I am still in a state of panic. I haven't been able to calm down since I got in here.*

Dr. Roberta: *Good. That makes my job easier. I want you to be upset and frightened. This method works only when your fear is readily apparent. In fact, I want you to think about dogs or about a specific dog and I want you to rate your fear. Think of a report card with grades A through F. A represents your being fine with a dog, F is you having a serious panic episode. Where are you right now?*

Andrew: *Well, a few minutes ago I was at F but now I'm somewhere between F and D.*

Dr. Roberta: *Is it fair to call it a D minus?*

Andrew: *Yes. That's it.*

Dr. Roberta: *Would it be accurate for you to say, I am terribly afraid of dogs?*

Andrew: *Yes. That's an understatement.*

Dr. Roberta: *Now, please repeat this sentence after me: Even though I am terribly afraid of dogs I am OK.*

At this point in the session Andrew repeated the sentence several times and then we began tapping. We went through the entire sequence of spots. Andrew said the full sentence when he tapped on the Karate spot and when he rubbed the Pledge spot. Then he simply said the word *dog* when tapping on the other spots.

We went through the entire sequence twice and Andrew reported that his D minus had turned into a B. At that point I asked him to identify the tapping spots that he thought were most helpful. He said the V Spot, Collarbone, Side, and Under-Eye. I suggested that he tap only those spots. He did and he got to an A after just one round of tapping. I like my clients to end with Karate spot taps, so he did that, although he claimed he didn't need to do any more tapping. He was flabbergasted at his progress, but then said: "Maybe this is working because I am in here and there are no dogs here. Maybe my phobia will return as soon as I step outside."

I had prepared for this possibility by alerting my neighbors. I told Andrew that my next-door neighbor had a dog and I suggested we go outside and ring their bell. Andrew, who just a few minutes before could barely walk from his car to my door, was eager to get going. He easily left the office and calmly stood at my neighbor's front door, hoping the dog was at home. We entered their living room and Andrew behaved like any guest would behave. We chatted a few minutes, he petted the pooch, and we left. Andrew called his mother when we got back to the office. He told her he was cured. She told him he was crazy. Six months later, as I write this book, Andrew continues to be cured.

FEARS AT DIFFERENT AGES

ACCORDING TO STUDIES, people experience different fears at different ages. For instance, youngsters are afraid of the dark, of strangers, and of medical procedures. Older people are afraid of crowds, accidents, illness, and separation. The majority of adults aged twenty to fifty who have phobias are fearful of enclosed spaces and of speaking in public. Are you nervous about presenting a report to a full group at your office? Are you anxious about making a sales presentation? Are you tense at the thought of speaking at your child's school conference? If you are a somewhat fearful person, *nervous*, *anxious*, and *tense* are considered normal emotional responses to these particular interpersonal situations. If, however, the thought of presenting a report at work convinces you to quit your job, or the thought of an upcoming sales meeting persuades you to change professions, or you consider home-schooling your child rather than participating in a parent conference, then you have a public speaking phobia.

True Report

MY BRAIN USED to go blank whenever my boss spoke to me. Even if he was just saying hello, I would stammer and sweat. Now, when I see him coming I take a deep breath and remember my three tapping spots and I am poised and prompt in my reply to him. I say hello as loud and clear as anyone. Sometimes I even make small talk and chat a bit with him. I've never actually tapped again after that first time. Now I just remember it.

—Tim

A FEAR OF PUBLIC SPEAKING

BARBARA OWNS A retail shop where she sells shoes and purses to fancy ladies. She easily communicates with her customers and has no trouble speaking one on one. She remembers that in school, years ago, she would feign illness and stay home whenever it was necessary for her to speak in front of her class. Thus, she avoided the situation that would provoke her fear and she thought nothing of it. She never considered that she might have a phobia because her life went along just fine.

For the past few years Barbara has donated merchandise to her town's homeless shelter. She developed a program for her customers, too. When they buy items from Barbara's store, she gives them a mail pouch for their purchase. Whenever they are ready to discard their shoes or bags, they slip them into the mail pouch, which is pre-addressed and postage-paid, and the items are delivered to the homeless shelter. Well, this year the shelter is honoring Barbara. They are holding a luncheon in her honor and she will be sitting up on the dais. She will be expected to make an acceptance speech when she is presented with her award.

Barbara is in a panic. She does not want to speak from the podium; in fact, she does not want to speak at all. Barbara came to me after two weeks of sleepless nights, loss of appetite, and fantasies about closing up shop and disappearing—all because she is phobic about public speaking.

When she walked into my office, Barbara seemed ill. She was too thin and looked exhausted. She confessed that she was serious about leaving town. The celebration in her honor was one week away. Barbara said, "Maybe it's time for me to take a long vacation. I will not show up at my luncheon. I can't. But then I'll be so embarrassed. I see no solution other than escaping for a long, long time."

I asked her to rate her fear, report-card style, on a scale of A through F. "No problem," Barbara said, "I know I am an F."

We got right to work. *I am afraid of speaking in public* was her basic sentence. We expanded it to: *Even though I am afraid of speaking in public I am OK.* Barbara was unable to say these words aloud. We actually had to change the sentence to: *Even though I am afraid of speaking in public I accept myself.*

Barbara was unable to say that she was OK, because her anxiety over this issue clearly disrupted her life and as she sat before me she was not OK. With some prodding from me, she was able to say that she would accept herself. Even so, the words seemed false to her, and it was only with great difficulty and after many attempts that she could actually utter the sentence. She chose the key word *speaking*.

I asked her to permit me to tap on her. She didn't look like she had the strength to tap herself. I began with her Karate spot while we both said the words of the sentence. Then she rubbed her Pledge spot, saying the sentence a little more clearly. I tapped all her spots. Barbara appeared startled. "What happened?" she asked. "I don't feel shaky."

"Good," I replied, "now you can do the tapping yourself." Barbara tapped. She went down to a B. She began to mutter to herself. I heard her say, "Why do some people think public speaking is a chore? I guess I was one of those people, huh? What happened? I don't get it."

Barbara continued to tap, reached an A, and then talked to me about her willingness to show up and speak at next week's luncheon. I mentioned that she had nothing to worry about, because in the worst case she could always tap herself while seated up on the platform. No one would be the wiser. The spots that worked best for her were Under-Eye, Collarbone, and Side. She could easily tap those spots, just a few seconds on each, without drawing any attention to herself. Barbara looked at me in amazement. "Why would I need to tap?" she exclaimed. "All I'm doing is getting up to speak for a few minutes. I don't want to make this into a federal case."

The Tapping Cure has the ability to completely remove a negative feeling from a thought. The thought of speaking in public no longer had any negativity attached to it, so the idea of being concerned about her upcoming speaking debut seemed ridiculous to Barbara. I conducted a mental rehearsal with her. She closed her eyes and imagined herself walking to the microphone, actually speaking, and then walking back to her seat. Throughout the visualization process she remained calm and thoroughly in control of herself and her feelings. When you rehearse a situation in your mind and are successful at it, you are very likely to repeat that success in real life.

YOUR TURN

Do you have a phobia? Approximately 12.5 percent of the U.S. population—that means more than 12 out of every 100 people—suffers from a phobia at some point in their lives. Do you have acrophobia—fear of heights? Do you have one of the newest phobias—cyberphobia—which is fear of computers? Yes, some people, admittedly very few, are extremely frightened of computers and will not work in an office where they will have to see one.

Then, of course, they cannot go to a doctor who has a computer in the office. Nor can they go to a library, a classroom, a sales office, etc. In fact, that's when they call me, because the fear has become a phobia and is taking over their life.

CAN YOU GUESS what these phobias are? (The answers appear at the bottom of the box.)

1. Triskadekaphobia _____
2. Phasmophobia _____
3. Claustrophobia _____
4. Iatrophobia _____
5. Acrophobia _____
6. Thalassophobia _____
7. Agoraphobia _____
8. Selenophobia _____
9. Pogonophobia _____

Answers: 1. fear of the number 13; 2. fear of ghosts; 3. fear of confined spaces; 4. fear of going to a doctor; 5. fear of heights; 6. fear of the ocean; 7. fear of public places and open spaces; 8. fear of the moon; 9. fear of beards.

SIMPLE PHOBIA

LET'S WORK ON your phobia now. If it is a simple phobia—that is, if it was not caused by trauma or by complicated circumstances, it will quickly and easily respond to tapping.

Can you come up with a sentence for you to tap on to get rid of your phobia? If it is a simple phobia, just fill in the blank: *Even though I am afraid of _____ I accept myself.*

Please get yourself upset and frightened and phobic. Become as scared as possible, without harming yourself. Think of confronting your fear. Feel the fright. Feel the terror, if you can bear it. If not, stop just short of the terror.

What report-card letter are you now? If you are at an F, that's wonderful. If you are not up at an F, please try to get there. Now please come up with a key word. On your piece of paper you should have your sentence, your key word, and your letter grade. Excellent.

Now you can begin your tapping sequence. Start with the Karate spot and say the entire sentence two times. Say it again while you rub the Pledge Spot. Now say your key word while you go through the entire tapping sequence once. Pause, take a deep breath, and assign yourself a new report-card letter. If you've gone down a letter or two, that is excellent. Just keep on doing what you are doing. Tap again and maybe once more after that. Good. You will soon be at an A. You will have cured your phobia with the Tapping Cure.

WISE WORDS

The wise man in the storm prays to God, not for safety from danger, but deliverance from fear.

—Ralph Waldo Emerson

Sometimes, when constructing your sentence for curing your phobia, you may find it necessary to do what Barbara did and replace *I am OK* with *I accept myself.* Self-acceptance may be important to you if you have a phobia, because you may have trouble accepting the phobic part of yourself. Probably, though, you feel fine about all other parts of yourself. Remember, we said that people with phobias are usually quite healthy and happy in other aspects of their lives. So, you already know that you are OK and therefore saying *I am OK* is not useful.

True Report

THE THOUGHT OF leaving town and going on a vacation is not a problem anymore. I don't worry beforehand like I used to. I tap my collarbones, both of them, with both hands, if I ever feel nervous about it. Ever since that tapping day in your office I never have to tell my boyfriend to cancel my ticket. I used to do that all the time.

—Daryl

COMPLICATED PHOBIA

SOME PHOBIAS ARE complex and stem from multiple intricate causes. When Mr. Hogan called, I suspected he would not be easy to work with. He told me that he had just been promoted and was phoning me from his expansive desk, facing huge windows offering a panoramic view of the city below. He had a new position at the stock brokerage company for which he had worked for many years. He told me that ever since his promotion he'd been unable to work. He sat at his desk and stared out the window. When I wondered out loud if the view was too distracting for him, he denied that. He said that he could not do what he was supposed to do because he was afraid of his phone!

It all began, he explained, when he felt that maybe he didn't deserve his promotion. Then he started thinking that he definitely didn't deserve it and would soon be found out. His phobia began when he was scared to answer the phone. He was afraid of accepting a phone call from anyone at his firm. He was certain that at any minute, one of the other employees would call and say, "Hey there, Hogan, I know that you are a fraud and you don't belong at that big desk in that big office." And so Mr. Hogan did not answer the phone, was terrified when the phone rang, and by the time he came to see me wouldn't even answer the phone at home because he thought "they" would track him down at home, too.

Mr. Hogan's phobia escalated from a fear of answering the phone at work to a fear of answering the phone at home to fear of a telephone anywhere. He would not look at a phone, hold a phone, sit near a phone. Hogan was phone-phobic.

I spoke to Mr. Hogan to find out if there was a particular reason why he felt he didn't deserve his promotion. He assured me that he actually was the best person in the company for this position. So we tried tapping on: *Even though I think I'm not qualified for this job I am OK.* That didn't work at all. Then we tried tapping on: *Even though I am scared of the phone I am OK.* We even tried: *Even though I think I'm not qualified for this job I accept myself* and *Even though I am scared of all phones I accept myself.*

Mr. Hogan said he started out as an F and remained there. He thought maybe he might be a D minus after trying all of the sentences with several rounds of tapping. I suspected that we were tapping for the wrong things. Maybe this was not a phobia after all. Maybe something else was going on. So I asked him to talk about other times in his life when he felt he had gotten a reward that he didn't deserve. Bingo! Mr. Hogan's face suddenly turned red and he broke eye contact with me. He became visibly shaken.

Years ago, in junior high school, Mr. Hogan had run for school office. He won by a landslide and was thrilled but surprised. He wasn't expecting to win because he was running against a very popular eighth grader. One week into his victory Mr. Hogan was confronted by the principal. Some students had rigged the election. Those students wanted the popular kid to lose and found ways to tamper with the ballots. Hogan was angry at himself for not having realized that something was amiss. He felt betrayed. He had been used by the students to further their own mean-spirited agenda. After all these years he was still angry at himself for not having figured out what had happened.

Mr. Hogan's phone phobia was really a complicated situation encompassing far more than a simple fear. He and I figured out that when the shenanigans were revealed all those years ago, he had felt many emotions—particularly embarrassment, anger, and betrayal.

Now we went through the tapping with new sentences. We didn't talk about phones or phobias. Instead we said: *Even though I was betrayed by my classmates I am OK.*

Hogan's key word was *betrayal* and in just two sequences of tapping he went from F to A. When I talked about the situation to try to get him to think about it so we could tap about his embarrassment and his anger, he was unable to get beyond an A when rating the entire experience of the school election. Good, I thought, now the phobia sentence we used earlier will work. But when I suggested we tap for: *Even though I am scared of the phone I am OK,* Mr. Hogan couldn't get his letter rating above an A! His phone phobia was not a phone phobia at all. His inability to work in his new office looked like a phobia but it was actually a complicated emotional response that had more to do with a long-ago event than with the current situation. It was a pseudo-phobia with a true traumatic situation at the bottom of it. Once the trauma was tapped on, the "phobia" disappeared.

What does Mr. Hogan's story have to do with you? It demonstrates that if you cannot move from an F when you tap to get rid of your phobia, you may be tapping on the wrong sentence. There is probably another aspect to the situation or a memory of a strong emotion that has been reactivated. You do not have a simple phobia. You have a complicated phobia that needs a more comprehensive approach. See chapter 7 for other ideas of what to do when tapping does not work, and consider talking about your phobia to yourself or into a tape recorder. As you talk, you may remember some similar situations from the past that will lead you to tapping your phobia away.

Some phobias do have complicated roots. Another example of a complicated phobia is one where you are afraid of driving a car and the fear began after you were in a car accident. In this phobic situation, you will not only tap on: *Even though I am afraid to drive I am OK,* but you will add an additional tapping sequence for: *Even though I was in a car accident I am OK.*

If you develop a fear of enclosed places after being stuck in an elevator for several hours, you will need to tap on: *Even though I am afraid of small, closed-in places I am OK* and also on: *Even though I was trapped in an elevator I am OK.*

SECONDARY GAIN

SOMETIMES, THERE IS another reason why you cannot get rid of a phobia with your tapping sequence. Sometimes there may be a part of you that really wants to remain phobic. Laura is a good example. She came to my office saying that she needed a quick fix. She suddenly couldn't drive on a highway. On her way to work she'd break out in a cold sweat. Her legs would shake so that she'd have to stop driving and pull over. She said she had no trouble driving in her neighborhood or on any local streets. But as soon as she entered an expressway, highway, or parkway, she was in big trouble. Laura asked if I could give her the Tapping Cure so that she wouldn't need to take any more leave from her job. She had no more sick days or personal days left. She came up with the sentence: *Even though I am scared of driving on a highway I am OK.*

She stayed at a D.

When several variations of this sentence didn't make any difference, I knew it was time for us to talk. I asked Laura to tell me about her life. She mentioned that she was in the middle of a divorce and her husband was not offering the financial settlement that she had hoped for. I asked Laura if the judge would award her more money if she had no income. "Of course," was her reply. Another bingo! If Laura lost her job because she could not drive to work, she would have no income during the course of the divorce negotiations and she would prosper financially. If she continued to work, she would receive almost nothing from her wealthy husband.

Laura and I talked about this, and she denied deliberately causing her driving problems. I agreed with her. Consciously, she wanted to drive. But sometimes people have trouble getting rid of a symptom because they derive a *secondary gain* from it. A secondary gain is an advantage that the symptom confers upon them. This is an unconscious mechanism that they are not aware of. On a conscious level, they do not see the relationship between their symptom and other life events. Laura's secondary gain is apparent. I suggested that she speak to her lawyer and then perhaps a psychotherapist. I assured her that when the divorce was final, she'd be able to drive. In the rare circumstance where she might not be able to resume highway driving, one brief tapping sequence would surely suffice.

If you suspect you are gaining an unconscious advantage by remaining phobic, you might want to tap on: *Even though I don't want to stop being afraid of _____ I am OK.*

Sometimes this does the trick. For Laura, above, her sentence would be:

Even though I don't want to stop being afraid of highway driving I am OK.

I like to tell my clients that even though they are feeling scared, it's possible for happiness to come their way. When you are in the midst of a phobic reaction it's useful to remember that when the object of your phobia is absent you are as calm and confident as ever.

A FEAR OF FLYING

FEAR OF FLYING is a phobia from which many people suffer. Often, this phobia does not really impact their lives until a family event or business obligation forces the issue. The actress Maureen Stapleton would not fly, but managed to have a full life on the New York stage and the Hollywood screen by relying upon cross-country railroads.

What about you? Are you like my client Rita? Rita, a devoted wife and mother, avoided flying while her children were small by insisting on local family vacations. When the children got older, the vacations were farther away and the car rides became longer and longer. Her loving husband understood and accommodated her need to avoid traveling by plane. Rita rarely thought about her fear; she had a good life. Everything changed when her son Eric met Laurie. Laurie loved Eric and Eric loved Laurie. They wanted to marry. Rita loved Eric. Rita loved Laurie. But, as wedding plans progressed, Rita wanted to disappear from the face of the earth. Rita and her family lived in New Jersey. Laurie is from Las Vegas. Her family, including cousins, aunts, uncles, grandparents, as well as parents, one sister, and two brothers, all lived in Las Vegas. The wedding would be in Las Vegas. Rita had been in a state of dread ever since Eric and Laurie had announced their engagement. She was tempted to bribe them to elope. As a last resort, she appeared in my office.

Hot Spots

Sometimes phobias can be rapidly cured by tapping Under-Eye, Collarbone, Side, V, and then a repeat: Under-Eye, Collarbone, Side, V. Sometimes you must also add Eyebrow One, Eyebrow Two, and Pinkie. Think of your fear while you tap.

Fear of flying is a simple phobia. It responds well to hypnosis and it responds well to the Tapping Cure. This sentence helped Rita, and it should also help you: *Even though I am afraid of flying I accept myself.* (Often, *I accept myself* works better than *I am OK* when curing phobias.)

This usually works like a charm. If it doesn't, then perhaps you didn't get yourself up to an F. Try again and be sure to think about your fear to the point of agitation. When your emotion is intense, your body and mind are receptive to being changed, and tapping is the way to make that change. After the Tapping Cure, Rita was no longer afraid of flying and began to look forward to the Las Vegas wedding.

In my experience, and in the experience of some of the pioneers of tapping, there are certain tapping spots that work particularly well for phobias. The best tapping spots for phobias, for most people, are:

- Under-Eye
- Collarbone
- Side
- V

As always, you begin by saying your full sentence two times while tapping the Karate spot and then while rubbing the Pledge spot. You may wish to end by tapping the Karate spot once again.

Of course you are invited to go through all the tapping spots and need not limit yourself to these. But this sequence should get rid of your phobia after just a few rounds of tapping. If you don't get totally down to A, consider adding:

- Eyebrow One
- Eyebrow Two
- Pinkie

Now that you can fly with ease, pay attention to your fellow passengers. You will notice people tapping! Invariably I see folks sitting in the terminal nonchalantly placing their chin in their cupped hand and tapping under their eyes. And during takeoff and landing I've observed Collarbone tappers and V spot tappers.

SUCCESS

You'll know you've succeeded in eradicating your fear when you think about it and can honestly say:

- It's no big deal
- I can handle it
- It no longer disturbs me

When you evaluate yourself on your report card you will be an A every time.

If you are among the one out of every eight people who suffers from a phobia, please suffer no more. You can tap away your fear. Your phobia will dissolve and your life will flourish. If by some remote chance your phobia persists, please go to a traditional mental health practitioner who will use exposure therapy. In time you will be relieved of your phobia. Good luck.

Remember This

PHOBIAS ARE CURABLE. The Tapping Cure usually does the trick. In case it doesn't, then go to a traditional psychologist, who will use exposure therapy—a time-tested type of therapy that gets good results. You deserve to be free of your phobia.

Tapping at Work and at Play

YOUR TAPPING SKILLS will help you negotiate tricky situations in the course of your daily life. You can be cool, calm, and collected under all circumstances.

TAPPING AT WORK

SOMETIMES YOUR PERFORMANCE at work reflects your emotional state. Did you ever notice that there are times when you cannot accomplish what you set out to do even though you know very well what needs to be done and how to do it? That's usually because your mind is busy dealing with an unresolved emotional issue. Your energy is being used up, unconsciously, and is not available to help execute the plans at hand. Tapping can help.

SUSAN'S WRITER'S BLOCK

Susan called me in a panic. She couldn't seem to get beyond chapter 4 of her novel-in-progress. Her publisher was waiting. Her agent was waiting. Her editor was waiting. Susan told me she would sit in front of her computer screen for hours. No words appeared; she simply couldn't continue writing. She was blocked. Also, she was desperate; her unpaid bills were rapidly accumulating.

We formulated a sentence: *Even though I feel uncreative and unimaginative I am OK.*

It did no good.

We talked more and came up with: *Even though I am cooped up and lonely in my small apartment I am OK.* Still no change. Her D remained a D. We talked some more and she expressed her fear of writing a novel that might not sell as well as her previous books. Now we were on to something and her new sentence was: *Even though I am a perfectionist I can continue writing and I will be OK.*

Susan's key word was *perfectionist*. Susan rated herself an A after a few rounds of tapping all her spots using this key word. I suggested that she tap every morning when she entered her writing room. I didn't hear from her after she left, but months later received an invitation to her book party.

Are You a Perfectionist?

If you are having trouble completing an assignment, or maybe even beginning that assignment, could it be that you are expecting too much of yourself? Are you assuming that you must be perfect? Most of us wouldn't attempt to do anything if we thought that the results must be flawless. Human beings tend to make mistakes. Help yourself accept your humanness by tapping on your perfectionism when necessary. You'll probably think of a sentence that suits you very well, but if you need some help to get started, consider: *Even though I'm not perfect I accept myself.*

True Report

MY DEADLINES AT work aren't scaring me anymore. I'm prepared for my meetings well in advance. When I'm coming up on a time limit and I think I am going to get clutched, I do my full taps two times and say: *Even if I'm slow I'm still a success.* I can't imagine why that helps me, but it always does. In fact, right after I do those taps I get to work and am very productive and not slow at all. Go figure.

—Mark

ERIK AND THE DOCTORS

Erik is a thirty-year-old man who has trouble at his hospital job. He's a physical therapist and works well with his patients. He knows how to do rehabilitation work and he knows how to get the patients motivated. But he runs into difficulty when it's time for him to give the physicians a progress report on their patients. He fumbles, blushes, and speaks unclearly when he's face to face with doctors. A couple of years of psychotherapy have helped him figure out why doctors bring out such feelings of self-consciousness in him, but his behavior persists nevertheless. Finally, realizing that insight is insufficient, Erik came to my office. He tapped on: *Even though I get rattled by doctors I am OK.*

He went from a D to a B. We couldn't get him down to an A so we talked some more. He mentioned that the Mustache spot seemed the most useful to him, so he tapped there for about thirty seconds before and after doing the full sequence of tapping spots. It worked! One of his co-workers, about six weeks later, asked Erik if he could let him know what tranquilizers he was taking—he so envied his composure.

If you have trouble communicating at work, consider tapping for a minute before you approach someone. If you don't have a minute, then just tap as long as you can on your Mustache spot.

Hot Spots

Need a quick dose of self-confidence? Use your fingers to tap on your Mustache spot and you'll feel ready to take on the world.

EMILY AND THE PATIENTS

Emily works in a clinic where she does occupational therapy with patients who've had serious shoulder surgery. An excellent clinician who communicates well with the doctors, Emily's challenge is to remain strong when her patients beg her to stop. Shoulder rehab is painful but necessary. Emily felt close to tears too often during her workday and knew that she needed some extra strength to be able to continue at the job she really loved. We came up with: *Even though it hurts me to see my patients in pain I am OK.*

It was successful right away. Emily tapped on all the tapping spots three times, beginning and ending with the Karate spot.

When you are in situations where you need extra courage, consider tapping a full sequence; if one spot was particularly helpful, go back and repeat it.

Wise Words

If you have a job without aggravations you don't have a job.

—Malcolm Forbes

COLD CALLS

Frank has to approach people who don't want to be approached. It's his job, as an insurance salesman, to sell them a policy that he believes is for their own good. Frank makes the first move, and then an appointment is set up. Once he goes to meet potential clients, what usually happens is that they are grateful for his attention and skill and they buy the policy. But Frank needs to make that initial phone call to set up the first meeting. Frank said to me, "Sometimes I get nervous about making those calls. I'll find so many things to do instead of getting to work. I'll send an e-mail to my sister in Chicago or I'll clean out the refrigerator, and once I actually picked up a poetry book from high school and decided I had to read it. Why can't I set up my appointments?"

We talked and decided to try a couple of possibilities. Perhaps Frank wants to avoid rejection, and when making cold calls it is a fact that a huge percentage of the folks answering the phone will say no. Possibly Frank doesn't like being perceived as rude, yet when he calls potential customers he is interrupting them. And the final possibility we thought we'd try was that perhaps Frank did not have answers to the many potential questions he might be asked about particular insurance policies.

Frank rated himself a D when assessing how he felt about sitting in front of the phone, taking out his call list, and beginning his work. Then he rated himself for each of his sentences individually. His sentences were: *Even though I may be rejected I'm OK* (rated F); *Even though some people may think I am rude I'm OK* (rated D); and *Even though I may not know everything about every policy I'm OK* (rated D minus).

Frank tapped a full sequence for the first sentence. He began with saying the entire sentence while tapping the Karate spot and the Pledge spot, and then he used the key word *rejected* while tapping on all the other spots. After one round he was down to a B and after a second he said he was at an A minus. We left it at that and went on to the second sentence, for which he chose the key word *rudeness*, and the third sentence, key word *smart*. The second sentence quickly became an A but the third sentence remained at a B. He said he felt much better and probably could buckle down to work with no problem. I suggested we try to figure out yet another sentence related to his knowledge of the policies. I thought this might be necessary because he had chosen the key word *smart*. Perhaps that indicated something more than not knowing about the policies. I suggested he tap on: *Even though customers may stump me with questions I will be successful.*

Bingo! An immediate A. To reinforce this, I reminded him that a smart person knows how and where to find the right answer. Frank liked that and asked if he could tap on: *Even though I may not know all the answers I know how to find the answers.*

That final sentence empowered him and he was eager to get to the phone. When you formulate your sentences, individualize the endings to suit your needs. Sometimes you'll do better with more than *I'm OK* at the end.

When I followed up with Frank about six months after his office visit, he told me that although he feels confident, he continues to tap every day, just in case. Although it's not necessary, there's no harm in continuing to tap after you're cured. It only takes a minute, and if it makes you feel even more secure, then go right ahead.

Wise Words

Boxer Muhammad Ali, former world heavyweight champ, always boasted. His mantra was "I am the greatest." His self-confidence was such that once, when asked how he was at golf, he replied, "I'm the best. I just haven't played yet."

TAPPING AT PLAY

Robin is a high school student who is dancing in the senior class recital. She told me that during rehearsals, her performance ranged from not so good to excellent. She asked if I could help her consistently achieve excellence. What she was asking for was *peak performance.*

PEAK PERFORMANCE

You know when you are doing your very best, be it at dancing or sports or playing an instrument. It feels like your body is simply proceeding on automatic. That's when you are going with the flow; you are in "the zone"—you are producing peak performance. During peak performance you are alert, but calm and confident. You are totally absorbed in what you are doing and you are enjoying yourself.

Two steps prepare you for peak performance.

Step One

First you tap, using whichever sentence is most appropriate for you. For Robin the sentence that worked was: *Even though I may not always be excellent at dance I am OK.* When you formulate your sentence, don't be afraid to go even further than *I may not always be excellent.* You can say: *Even though I may never be a good dancer I am OK* or *Even though I am a bad dancer I am OK.*

You may prefer ending your sentence with *I accept myself.*

The tapping spots that worked best for Robin, and usually work well with performers and athletes, are: Eyebrow One, Eyebrow Two, Under-Eye, and V.

Step Two

After tapping, it is useful to do a mental rehearsal. Mental rehearsal is the process of visualizing yourself achieving your goal. Robin saw herself on the stage, in the auditorium, dancing perfectly. In her mind she heard the music, saw the other dancers, watched herself, and visualized the audience, too. When you do a mental rehearsal, engage all your senses. See the entire area, feel the weather—are you hot? Are you cold? Is there a breeze? Are you in a stuffy room? Hear all the sounds and noises, and smell all the smells.

Bob Reese, former trainer for the New York Jets, says, "There is no guarantee that if you create a vision it will happen. But there is a guarantee that if you don't have a vision, it will never happen."

Mental processes at work during mental rehearsal actually affect your body. When you intensely visualize yourself performing an activity, subtle changes can occur in the very muscle groups that would have been activated had you actually performed the motions you visualized. Some studies have indicated that actions learned by visualization are retained even better than actions learned by actual performance. Visualization is an established part of athletic-team training these days.

Tap and visualize, and you will be on your way to peak performance.

Hot Spots

Peak performance can be attained when you tap Eyebrow One, Eyebrow Two, Under-Eye, and V, and then repeat the sequence. Do a mental rehearsal and you'll be good to go.

TEAM SPORTS

If you are nervous before a game and want to gain confidence, consider tapping before going out on the field. Run through all your tapping spots while saying (to yourself if there's no privacy): *Even though I am nervous I'm OK* or *Even though I'm nervous I'm a great player.*

Use the key word *game* or *ballgame* or *team*.

SOCIAL SITUATIONS

OTHER PEOPLE CAN give you cause to feel upset. But now that you know how to tap, you have the ability to rapidly extinguish any negative feelings. Perhaps you identify with some of the clients described below who have trouble in social situations.

True Report

When I'm about to leave the apartment to go to meet new people in a social situation, well, you know what I mean, in a bar, I tap before I leave the house. I stand in front of the mirror and say: *Even though I'm shy I am very likable*, while I tap all the spots. As soon as I finish doing that, I am ready to rock. I'm not sure if I'm shy anymore, either, but I still say it.

—Joseph

RED-FACED

Debra is a thirty-five-year-old airline pilot who came in for a consultation wondering if anything could be done about her perpetual blushing. Debra complained that in the course of normal conversation—not only with strangers but also with people she knows—she often feels herself blush and knows that her face becomes lipstick-red.

Going through the tapping spots once and then twice changed her grade about talking to people in regular conversations from an F to a D. Not very useful. I asked Debra if she could recall the first time she experienced that embarrassed feeling that produced the blushing. She remembered exactly where and when it had occurred. There was a misunderstanding when Debra was a child, and she was wrongfully accused of a minor crime. Although she was quickly exonerated, the deep feelings of shame persisted. Today she continues to blush whenever she suspects someone does not fully understand her. She blushes if she believes someone might misinterpret her acts or her words.

Can you think of a good sentence for Debra to tap on? Debra thought of two: *Even though I blush I am OK* and *Even though I was falsely accused I accept myself.*

We began with the usual two beginning spots—the Karate spot and the Pledge spot. Then we did the full array of spots. Debra said she was down to a B. She said she felt that she had gotten extreme relief from the Mustache, Collarbone, Pinkie, and V spots. Those were the spots she did twice each; then she did the Karate spot as an ending. Debra was at A.

If you need to deal with issues of embarrassment or shyness, consider trying these four spots first. Perhaps they'll solve your problem without you needing to tap all the other spots.

Hot Spots

Embarrassed? Shy? Many folks have success when tapping on Middle, Collarbone, Pinkie, and then V.

LOW SELF-ESTEEM?

DO YOU FEEL inadequate? Do you think you don't deserve to be happy? Does your personality hold you back socially? Do you think you don't deserve to be successful? Are you stuffed with self-doubt? Before we use tapping to overcome these false beliefs, please check out whether or not there is truth to your ideas about yourself. If many people corroborate that you are indeed inadequate and if they all believe that if you continue on the path you are following you may never be happy and never fulfill your plans, please don't try to tap for self-esteem. Instead learn some new skills and get some advice about new ways of behaving. You may need guidance to help yourself get up to speed in the areas where you are lacking. However, if you are the only one who believes you should fail at life, it's time to get over your low self-esteem.

Usually low self-esteem begins when wrong or false information is imparted to a child. You were once that child and you absorbed that false information and incorporated it into your self-perception.

Negative information has stickiness to it—it can stick to you for years and years and erroneously guide you as you make life choices.

More than once I've had a client who was able to trace low self-esteem back to a comment made quite casually by a parent. Children take in parental comments and hold on to them for decades. One man was told by his father that he had a speech impediment. In later years he realized he didn't; it was just normal childhood speech that his father thought was abnormal. Nevertheless the young man refrained from speaking up in class, did not accept a scholarship to law school, and, until he was twenty-four and figured out what was going on, he did not date for fear of being ridiculed when he spoke. (For the record, he spoke just fine.)

If you're lucky, you, too, will be able to figure out the false statement that was said to you and that shaped your self-perception. When you get that sentence in your mind, simply tap on it by adding *I now know the truth* to the end. A typical sentence might be: *Even though my mother told me I was ugly, I now know the truth.*

Thankfully, tapping can erase those wrong perceptions and you will be free to lead a good life and have good feelings about yourself. Before you begin, rate your feelings on the A to F scale. F is the worst possible self-esteem; A is when you hold yourself in high, respectful regard.

If you cannot recall a particular moment from your childhood, think about the areas in your life where you feel you do not measure up. Usually there are several. For the last part of your tapping sentence, you can replace *I am OK* with *I can succeed* or with *I now know the truth.* Some possible sentences:

- *Even though I am undeserving I can succeed* or *Even though I used to think I was undeserving I now know the truth*
- *Even though I am unattractive I can succeed* or *Even though I used to think I was unattractive I now know the truth*
- *Even though I am stupid I can succeed* or *Even though I used to think I was stupid I now know the truth*

- *Even though I am a disgrace I can succeed* or *Even though I used to think I was a disgrace I now know the truth*
- *Even though I am unlovable I can succeed* or *Even though I used to think I was unlovable I now know the truth*
- *Even though I am a bad person I can succeed* or *Even though I used to think I was a bad person I now know the truth*
- *Even though I am worthless I can succeed* or *Even though I used to think I was worthless I now know the truth.*

Use your tapping spots chart and begin with the Karate spot, and then rub the Pledge spot. Next tap on all spots. Your key word will depend upon the sentence you are using. After you reach an A, ask yourself if you feel ready to take on the world. If you don't, then find another sentence to tap on, and then another. When you finally cover all the issues, you'll be rid of the false information that has mistakenly been stuck to your personality. You will no longer have ideas about yourself that limit you. You will be on an equal playing field with everyone else. Many people say that the Mustache spot is extremely useful for clearing up issues of self-esteem. Try it and see if it works for you in addition to all the other spots. Or, you might find that you are full of self-confidence most of the time but in certain circumstances you need a boost. Discreet Mustache spot tapping might be your answer.

Hot Spots

For quick stress relief, tap Eyebrow One, Under-Eye, Side, and Collarbone, and then repeat.

ANXIETY

ARE YOU THE nervous type? Are you the one in your family who worries about everything and everyone? Do you have trouble in social situations because you are all jittery? Are *calm* and *relaxed* two terms that are rarely applied to you? If so, you are in luck. Tapping can eradicate anxiety symptoms. Most of us who use tapping with our clients know this to be true, and there is some hard scientific data that supports it, too.

As part of a research study in South America, tapping was used to treat tens of thousands of anxiety patients over a span of many years. Detailed records were kept, and the results are impressive. The study was conducted by a physician named Joaquín Andrade, at his eleven treatment centers in Uruguay and Argentina. Over the course of fourteen years, Dr. Andrade's thirty-six therapists treated twenty-nine thousand patients.

One study that involved five thousand patients was conducted as follows: whenever someone with anxiety symptoms or complaints of excessive nervousness showed up at particular clinics or medical centers, they were sent either to a tapping practitioner or to a cognitive behavioral therapist who used psychotherapy and prescribed medication, if needed. The patients were suffering from fears, separation anxiety, PTSD, feelings of panic, and overall nervousness.

A FEAR IS a thought about something in the present, while *anxiety* is usually a fear about something in the future. You are fearful when a bear is approaching you; you experience anxiety when you are told that bears have been spotted in the woods where you are hiking.

A team of evaluators interviewed each of these patients at different stages of their treatment and then several times after their treatment concluded. The evaluators had no idea whether the people they were interviewing had received tapping or traditional therapy. Here are the results at the end of treatment:

Psychotherapy patients:

63 percent had improved

51 percent were totally symptom-free

15 sessions were needed to get results

50 percent of the patients who were taking medications had side effects from their drugs.

Tapping patients:

90 percent had improved

76 percent were totally symptom-free

3 sessions were needed to get results

No medication used; no chance for reactions

In another study, this time of sixty-four patients who were treated for generalized anxiety disorder (GAD), of the thirty patients who were prescribed anti-anxiety drugs, 70 percent got better. Of the thirty-four patients who were tapped instead of medicated, 78 percent got better. Again, in this study, half of the medicated patients had bothersome side effects.

All the tapping spots were tapped upon in the treatment protocol.

Now you know that tapping can help you with your nervousness, your anxiety, and your panic reactions. To calm yourself and to develop an anti-stress routine, I suggest you tap this sequence: Karate spot, Pledge spot (rub, don't tap), all tapping spots, and then Karate spot again.

If you still feel anxious, try to figure out which spots were most useful to you. When did your mind and your body relax? Which spot were you tapping on when you took a good deep breath? In my practice I've noticed that certain people respond with serenity when they tap on Eyebrow One, Under-Eye, Side, and Collarbone. Experiment. See which of those spots works best for you. Maybe two or three or all four in a particular order will immediately cure you. Keep trying and you'll come up with your unique anti-stress tapping remedy. As mentioned earlier, the V Spot is good for calmness, too.

DOUBLE-BLIND STUDIES

ARE YOU WONDERING why the medical establishment doesn't see the experiments described above as proof of the value of tapping? Well, in order for studies to be deemed properly scientific, they must be done according to the strictest protocol. While the studies above were done well, they did not conform to U.S. standards; nor were they double-blind. A double-blind study would have offered tapping to a portion of the group, and offered another portion of the group a procedure that appeared to be the same as tapping (but actually was not). The second group actually receives a sham treatment. When the results are tallied, if patients in the tapping group are far more improved than patients in the sham group, it is clear that tapping was the successful intervention. Without the double-blind component, it is impossible to know if perhaps everyone would have improved anyway, with the passage of time, whether or not they were tapped.

A recent study that compared tapping with acupuncture was successful in promoting tapping but unsuccessful in getting professional recognition, again because it was not a double-blind study. The doctors treated patients with panic disorder. Forty patients were instructed to tap on particular acupuncture points. Thirty-eight patients received true acupuncture on those same points. Half of the acupuncture patients improved and had significantly fewer panic responses. Seventy-eight percent of the tapping patients improved and had significantly fewer panic responses.

Recently, serious medical double-blind experiments have changed the way doctors treat knee problems. For years, arthroscopic knee surgery was the norm for certain knee conditions. Some of the patients did well and others did not. Then a double-blind test was done and some patients actually got sham surgery. This took place at the Houston VA Medical Center and involved 180 knee patients. The results were reported in the July 11, 2002, issue of the esteemed medical publication *New England Journal of Medicine*. The patients who got the sham surgery were anesthetized in the operating room, and doctors poked around their knees. The other patients got real knee surgery. Two years later, when both groups of patients were evaluated and no one knew whether or not they had had the real surgery, it was determined that the same percentage of patients in each group considered their knee function recovered. Within the groups of those who received sham surgery and those who received real surgery, there were similar percentages of patients who were still in pain and those who were up and running. The double-blind study proved that arthroscopic knee surgery does not necessarily help. A knee may get better with time and with exercise, without surgery.

If a double-blind study were to indicate that tapping made no difference in the treatment of anxiety, because the same number of people who recovered using tapping could get better without tapping, would I think that no one should bother tapping anymore? I don't think so. Tapping does not require the services of highly paid surgeons and nurses; nor does it entail a hospital, anesthesia, or all the risks and expenses that go along with surgery. Tapping is about you, sitting in your living room, spending less than five minutes tapping yourself. That's a no-brainer; there is no downside to tapping, unless you are going to an enormously expensive practitioner rather than doing it yourself, or unless you are persisting in tapping and not seeing any improvement, in which case you need to consult a medical professional.

GENERALIZED ANXIETY DISORDER

GENERALIZED ANXIETY DISORDER (GAD) is a recognized medical problem. The following are signs of GAD:

- You worry a lot
- You cannot control your worrying

- Your worrying interferes with your daily functioning
- You have at least three of the following symptoms, too: irritability, muscle tension, trouble sleeping, trouble concentrating, fatigue, and restlessness

If you've just diagnosed yourself with GAD, you've probably been nervous most of your life and have inherited this condition from one of your parents or grandparents. Your disorder probably gets worse during times of additional stress.

Now you have a name for your condition, and now it's time to cure it. Tapping may do the trick. Tap every day. Tap for different circumstances. Tap when you are about to go somewhere. Tap when your thoughts are bothering you. After a week of tapping, you should see some spectacular results. If you don't, then please go to a doctor. There is no need for you to suffer. GAD is a treatable disease.

If you are a worrywart, you will feel better after you tap. Tap on the full range of tapping spots and tap for every worry you have. At first, like Nadine, below, you might need to tap many, many times every day. That's OK. Soon your worries will diminish, and you'll be tapping less and less. Many GAD sufferers are helped by tapping on all their spots at first and then on only Under-Eye, Collarbone, and Side. Try it.

NADINE

Nadine introduced herself to me and immediately stated that she was just like her mother—a worrywart. She worried when she woke up in the morning—would she get the kids off to school OK? Did she plug in the coffeepot for her husband? Does her sweater need to be ironed? She worried during the day—what should she prepare for dinner? What if there's no time to help her daughter with homework? What if her son gets a low mark on his math test? What if she misses the call from her sister-in-law about next week's celebration? Nadine tapped for every little worry. She tapped for every big worry. I encouraged her to tap every time her mind began to worry. She tapped many, many, times each day. After about six days Nadine called to say she had fewer things to tap for. She came back to my office two weeks later and said that her worrying during the day was pretty much gone. Now she worried only in the evenings. This was an improvement, but not good enough. I asked her to keep a record of her worries. Every time a disturbing thought popped into her mind, she was to write it down. When it reached twenty thoughts I told her to start tapping. She tapped on one of those thoughts each day. At the end of three more weeks, all items on that list no longer bothered her. A typical tapping sentence for Nadine is: *Even though I am afraid my daughter will get hurt on her way home from school I will be OK.*

If you are like Nadine, please tap as often as you can. Your mind will become soothed and soon you will have less and less to worry about and less and less to tap about. I closely monitored Nadine with phone calls. Had she not shown improvement, I definitely would have referred her to a medical doctor. GAD is a troublesome condition and it is wrong to suffer from it. You can eliminate it and you should eliminate it.

Hot Spots

GAD (generalized anxiety disorder) and OCD (obsessive-compulsive disorder) are often helped by tapping Under-Eye, Collarbone, and Side.

OBSESSIVE-COMPULSIVE DISORDER

DO YOUR WORRIES become obsessions? Some people have obsessive-compulsive disorder. If you do and if the obsessive part of the disorder is most prominent, then you will have persistent thoughts, images, and ideas that you cannot get out of your head. If the compulsions are the most prominent parts of your disorder, then you will feel compelled to do certain actions over and over. Some repetitive behaviors are excessive praying, excessive hand-washing, excessive counting, and excessive checking. You might also have some rigid rules you believe you must obey even though you don't want to because they interfere with your day. Such a rule may be having to walk around your chair thirteen times before you can sit in it, or wearing gloves to protect your fingers from germs that no one else seems concerned about, or arranging your personal effects in a particular order that takes up far too much time.

OCD does not respond to logical persuasion, but often responds to medication and also to tapping. Collarbone, Under-Eye, and Side are the spots recommended. Try tapping on all three in any sequence you wish, while you say: *Even though I feel compelled to* _____*I'm OK* or *Even though I feel compelled to* _____ *I like myself.*

You are unique. You may respond best to tapping on all tapping spots or on just a few. Please take the time and trouble to experiment. You will identify your best tapping spots.

Remember This

TAPPING CAN HELP you every day. Life can be easier when you tap. Try it at work and try it at play. Nervousness is not a necessary state of being. If tension and anxiety are in your genetic makeup, your daily life is compromised, your relationships are compromised, and your energy level is compromised. Tapping can free you. And, best of all, you can tap yourself in public—say only your key word, not the entire sentence—and no one will notice.

Annoyance, Anger, Guilt, and Other Everyday Emotions

*I*T'S A SAD fact of life that you cannot control what other people do or what other people say. But, with tapping, you can control *your* reaction to other people's actions and words. You can control your response to whatever may be going on in your life.

ANNOYED?

THE TAPPING CURE works well for life's little annoyances. You know what I mean—the irritability you feel when your buddy is late for your morning walk, whereas you rushed to get to the track on time; the tension you feel when your physician says he'll give you the results of your annual physical, but the waiting room is packed. You are rightfully annoyed, but you don't want to react childishly. You want to handle your emotions with maturity.

You will get relief from troubles and increase your coping ability by tapping on the full sequence of spots. If you wish, though, there are some spots that some people feel are more likely to help with specific situations. For example, to cope with frustration and to increase your patience, tap Eyebrow One, Eyebrow Two, Under-Eye, and Collarbone. Those are the spots that for most people provide immediate calm when they are faced with a frustrating circumstance (waiting on line at the motor vehicle bureau, trying to get the attention of the salesclerk who is on the phone, getting stuck in traffic, sitting next to a loudmouth at a party).

If you've noticed a better tapping spot, a spot that consistently changes your mood and puts you into a relaxed state, then certainly add it to the mix and tap on it. You don't have to make a big deal about your tapping. Whether you're standing on the track or sitting in your doctor's waiting room, subtle tapping is not noticeable at all. Just a few seconds on each spot should do the trick.

While you tap, permit yourself to feel the full extent of your annoyance, of your anger. You can rate your feeling state using the A to F scale to yourself, just so you'll be sure to know how rapidly you are improving. And then say an appropriate sentence. If you're in public, say it to yourself. When you're annoyed at having to wait for your tardy friend, you might say:

Even though my friend is keeping me waiting I am OK.

Your key word might be *waiting.*

If you are nervous while waiting for your blood test results from your doctor you might tap on: *Even though I feel nervous about what I'll be told I am OK.*

Your key word might be *doctor.*

Use these suggested tapping spots as starting points, but feel free to experiment. Perhaps you'll need just one of these spots to decrease your impatient feelings. Or maybe you'll add one or come up with a totally different combination of tapping spots. You will find a way to easily tolerate situations that heretofore would have irritated you. After tapping, you may find yourself thinking, *What's the big deal? I am OK.*

Hot Spots

Are you irritable? Are you cranky? For some people, rubbing the Pledge spot is sufficient to take care of irritability, and no tapping at all is needed. Try it! While you rub, say a sentence about what is bothering you, ending the sentence with *and it's no big deal*.

If you are often annoyed and often irritated by others, you might want to get checked out by a physician. Sometimes irritability is caused by an undiagnosed illness—maybe a depression or a thyroid disorder—and sometimes it is caused by lack of sleep. If everything checks out fine, then you know that your irritability is in response to something that has occurred. You have a choice, you know. You can respond to an event in a variety of ways. You can respond with a calm attitude. You can respond by telling yourself that everything is OK or will be OK. You can tap at the same time that you give yourself the message that all will be well. Tapping will ensure that the message is delivered to your brain. Experiment with all the tapping spots, and the next time you are about to become annoyed at something or someone, you'll surprise yourself, and others, by remaining in control of your emotions.

ANGRY?

WHAT IS MAKING you angry? Are you a stay-at-home mom whose children are insisting on your full attention so that you cannot accomplish anything on your to-do list? Are they making a mess in the kitchen? Are they whining to you and arguing with each other? Did your son just break a vase after you told him not to play with a ball in the house? Did your daughter tie up the phone and forget to give you that important message from the vet? Are you working in an office where the boss plays favorites and it's not you? Are you a team member whose teammates expect you to do their share of the work? Are you a friend who is expected to chauffeur around other friends?

If you are more than annoyed—if you are downright angry—then it's time to tap. Don't bother giving a letter value to your anger—you'll know right away when you are calm enough. You can go through all the tapping spots or you can use the spots suggested above, the ones for annoyances—Eyebrow One, Eyebrow Two, Under-Eye, and Collarbone—and then please add your Side spot after the collarbone, and repeat the entire sequence. Your sentence might be: *Even though the kids are driving me crazy I'm OK*, and your key word might be *kids*.

Some people get instant relief from feelings of anger by tapping Pinkie, Collarbone, V, Pinkie, Collarbone. Try a combination of all these spots to come up with the right ones for you. I recommend starting and ending with the Karate spot. Of course, at any time you can decide to tap on all of your tapping spots.

ENRAGED?

THERE'S A DIFFERENCE between being annoyed, being angry, and being enraged. Mr. Barnes, the owner of a successful business, is enraged.

Mr. Barnes: *I have coped with critical issues in my life, including the death of my first wife and some serious financial reversals. But I'm suffering more now than ever. Since my daughter's wedding I've not had one good night's sleep. I'm angry all the time. I go into rages at my office. My secretary is scared of me these days. I went to the cardiologist because of chest pain and he checked me out and said my heart is fine but I have bad anxiety. I know that, but I can't help it.*

Dr. Roberta: *What is it that's upsetting you so much?*

Mr. Barnes: *It's my daughter. She's an idiot. Her husband married her for her trust fund. Anyone with half a brain could see that. But not her. She has a fancy education that I paid for with hard-earned bucks, yet she can't see what is obvious to everyone else.*

Dr. Roberta: *So, let's figure out what's going on here. What is really upsetting you? Is it your daughter's dubious taste in husbands? Is it the fact that you have to stand by and watch her make a mistake? Is it the issue of money? Is it that you have no control over your child?*

Mr. Barnes: *Hmm, I guess it's not the money. I can always provide for her. It's the idea that someone is taking advantage of her—and that she loves him.*

Dr. Roberta: *Sometimes we have to watch our kids make mistakes. Hopefully they learn from their experience and they're young enough to change and overcome.*

Mr. Barnes: *My mind knows that. But not my chest. My heart pounds when I look at his face. I use all my self-control not to punch him out.*

I persuaded Mr. Barnes to think about how infuriated he was about his daughter and her husband. His bright red face told me he measured an F on the report card; I didn't need to ask. I directed him to say: *Even though I detest my son-in-law I'm OK* and then tap a full sequence of all spots. Immediately he seemed relaxed and in control of himself. I asked which tapping spots helped most. He identified the Pinkie spot and Eyebrow One and Eyebrow Two. He tapped those spots again a few times, and then ended with the Karate spot. Although Mr. Barnes left our session claiming to feel just fine and accepting of his daughter and her husband, I suggested that he tap before all family get-togethers, just to be on the safe side. I also suggested that he use the effective tapping sequence anytime he felt his heart racing or his face reddening.

The beauty of the Tapping Cure is that you can formulate it to meet your specific needs and you can do it whenever you wish. If you fly into rages, try to prevent them by tapping just before you are about to encounter a person or a situation that usually infuriates you. Use all of your tapping spots or concentrate on Pinkie, Eyebrow One, Eyebrow Two, Under-Eye, and Collarbone.

GUILTY?

MARY IS AN office worker known throughout her company and throughout her neighborhood as the "pet lady." You know the type. She takes in strays, she feeds the homeless, and there are many, many folks who rely on her acts of kindness.

One day when Mary visited her cousin, he commented that his dog was not doing well and said the vet thought it might be an intestinal problem. The vet cautioned the family against feeding the dog. "Starvation might cure the problem, food could make it much worse," he had said.

Mary's heart hurt when she saw the dog whimpering with pain and begging for food. When her cousin stepped out, Mary gave the dog some table scraps. Several hours later the dog died.

It was two months after the dog's death that Mary appeared in my office. Although her cousin had forgiven her, Mary was unable to forgive herself. She appealed to me to help her get on with her life and stop berating herself. She said her feelings of remorse were punishment enough; she did not want to hate herself forever. She did want to be able to resume life.

Her report card was an F when she said, *I killed the dog.*

The full sentence Mary wanted to say was *Even though I killed the dog I am OK.* I changed that to *Even though I accidentally killed the dog I am OK.*

It's true that she was warned not to feed the dog, but nevertheless she had good intentions; she was not planning to kill the dog, only to feed him.

Sometimes guilt is necessary; it can help maintain proper behavior in a society. Civilized people react with guilt when they break rules and exceed boundaries. That is a good thing. But when guilt paralyzes you and prevents you from enjoying life, it is time to settle the situation, learn from it, and tap to get over it. When you need to deal with guilt, consider tapping the Pinkie and Index spots first; then try Pinkie and Collarbone. You may not need to use all the others if a combination of those will work. But don't hesitate to use all spots if that works best for you. When you are tapping, remember to think about how guilty you feel.

Mary used the key word *dog* and tapped three times on all the tapping spots. She got down to a B and said the finger spots and Collarbone were the most helpful. Mary tapped on Pinkie and Index, back and forth a few times, adding the Collarbone at the end of each round, and got down to a solid A. I suggested she tap at home to: *Even though I accidentally killed the dog, that was in the past and it's over.*

Hot Spots

Guilt can be overcome by tapping on Pinkie and then either Index or Collarbone or both. Repeat the sequence several times.

OBSESSED?

MARLENE CAME TO my office convinced that she was guilty, but all our tapping didn't help. Finally, I realized that while she might have thought she was guilty, her real problem was an obsession. She could not stop thinking—obsessing—about a particular incident.

Marlene said, "My mind won't shut up. It won't turn off. I keep thinking I am responsible for my mother's death. I sent her aide with her in the ambulance and I stayed in bed. By the time I got to the hospital in the morning, she was gone. I feel so guilty."

One night, Marlene worked in her office quite late. She had taken a few hours off during the day to check on her mom in the nursing home, and she had to catch up on all the work on her desk. She became immersed in her work and it wasn't until 1:30 a.m. that she finally arrived home and went to bed. Marlene was exhausted and quickly fell into a deep sleep. Soon, though, she was startled awake by the ringing of the phone. It was her mother's aide calling from the nursing home to say that her mother's blood pressure had suddenly risen and the doctor on call wanted to hospitalize her. The aide said, "I'll go with the ambulance. The doctors think a few hours of IV medication should help and they'll begin it as soon as we get to the hospital."

Marlene was dead tired. She said, "OK. Thanks. Tell Mom I'll see her tomorrow." And then she rolled over and went right back to sleep. In the morning she planned to check in on her mom in the hospital, and then go in to her office. That was not to be. While she was driving to the hospital, Marlene's cell phone rang. "Come here immediately," shouted the aide. Marlene knew it was trouble. Sure enough, when she arrived there was a white sheet covering her mother's body. Her mother had died.

All Marlene could think at that moment was, "Why didn't I get up and go to the hospital during the night? Why did I stay in bed? I would have seen that something was wrong. I would have gotten the right help. I could have saved my mother, but instead I stayed in bed."

And a few days later Marlene was still saying, "I could have saved my mother, but instead I stayed in bed." And days turned into weeks and weeks turned into months. When she finally arrived at my office, after seeing her internist, a social worker, a psychiatrist, her rabbi, and a psychiatric nurse from the nursing home, eight months had passed. Eight months of anguish.

We talked. We tapped. We talked some more. And after the fourth round of tapping on: *Even though I slept while my mother was dying I accept myself* and *Even though that thought keeps whirling in my head I will be OK*, Marlene reported that she was a B plus. I suspected that she might not reach an A until the next day and instructed her to tap the next few days on: *Even though that thought sometimes whirls in my head I am OK.*

I called a week later and Marlene was symptom-free. In the two years since her appointment, Marlene's obsessive thoughts have never returned. She simply never thinks like that anymore.

If you, like Marlene, feel guilty about something that you cannot get out of your mind, tapping while thinking about your guilt may not be as useful as tapping while addressing the fact that the thought has now become an obsession.

You may not need all of the tapping spots. As always, you need to experiment and come up with the right combination of tapping spots for you. Perhaps you'll simply go through them all a couple of times and that will be sufficient. In my experience, certain spots work particularly well for obsessions, particularly Under-Eye and Collarbone, and sometimes Thumb and Side, too. Consider the following tapping sequence to get down to an A: Under-Eye, Collarbone, Thumb, Side, and V.

After a few rounds of these tapping spots, you will have no interest in the thought that had been haunting you. In fact, even when you try you'll be unable to think about it.

Hot Spots

Obsessions often respond to Under-Eye, Collarbone, Thumb, Side, and V. Do this sequence two times while concentrating on your obsession. It could be just the quick fix you need.

FULL OF HATE?

CLAIRE THOUGHT CONSTANTLY about her sister-in-law. She hated her sister-in-law. Claire insisted that her brother had married a gold digger who didn't care for him or love him at all.

"I am letting that gold digger ruin my life. I think about her all the time. I can't enjoy myself because she is on my mind. I seethe when I think of her, and I always think of her. She fills my mind with hate. I can't go on like this. Please help me."

Claire was suffering from an obsession and from hatefulness. We formulated three sentences:

- *Even though I hate Linda I am OK*
- *Even though my brother is married to Linda I am OK*
- *Even though Linda is after my brother's money I am OK*

Claire's key words were *hate, married,* and *money.* But she didn't have to do much tapping. After the first round, for the first sentence, she felt immediate relief and said that the Collarbone spot made all the difference. For the next two sentences Claire tapped only on her collarbone, and in less than one minute she was totally relaxed and accepting of her sister-in-law. When I tested her by suggesting that Linda might use up all of her brother's wealth, Claire replied, "I guess that's his problem, not mine. I didn't marry her, he did." Her hate had totally dissipated.

HEARTBROKEN?

IN THE COURSE of life you will probably experience a relationship that ends. It will end because you want it to end, because the other person wants it to end, or perhaps because of the death of the other person. Sometimes, even when it is your choice to end a relationship, you can feel heartbroken anyway. That's because it is not the end of the relationship that you are mourning—you really do not want to perpetuate a bad relationship—but the end of your special dream. Your future plans are gone; there is no hope for them. Also, you are mourning the familiar routine you established with that person. Fortunately, the Tapping Cure can help you deal with affairs of the heart. Read below about several clients who quickly tapped their way from inconsolable to joyful.

True Report

WHEN I WALKED into your office I was sure I could not go on living. Mickey had left me and my life was over. When I walked out of your office it was hard to remember why I'd ever cared about that jerk. I must admit that I am afraid my feelings may return, so just to be sure I tap for two minutes every night before I go to sleep. I love tapping! I have no feelings for Mickey. None at all.

—Jan

BROKEN UP

Vicki held back her tears. She whined and whimpered and said, "I'm a worthless person. I don't know why I decided to break up with Brian. Now I am all alone. I hate being alone. I have no boyfriend and that is too awful. I miss him and I shouldn't have told him it was over. He was my good friend. Can you help me? I am miserable. I hate myself because of this. It was the worst decision of my life."

Interestingly, Vicki initiated the breakup, but now feels she is diminished as a human being because she is without a boyfriend. Her letter rating was an F and she cried while she tapped. We tapped on: *Even though I broke up with Brian I am OK.*

No effect.

We tapped on: *Even though I broke up with Brian I will be OK.*

No effect.

We tried: *Even though I broke up with Brian I accept myself.*

Still no effect.

We talked and talked, and finally Vicki revealed that her roommate Katherine had expressed an interest in Brian and now was dating him.

This time we tapped on: *Even though Brian is with Katherine, I accept myself and I am OK.*

We went through all the tapping spots for this one. Vicki experienced quick relief. After one round of tapping, she thought she was an A or maybe a B plus. There was not one spot that seemed more useful than any other. We chatted a while and then I asked Vicki to visualize Brian with Katherine and let me know how upset she felt.

Vicki: *I'm an A, I guess. I can't really think about them. My mind is filled with many lovely and more important things to think about. There's no room in there for them.*

Dr. Roberta: *Concentrate on the image of Brian coming into your apartment, but to be with Katherine, not you. What letter comes to mind? How upset are you?*

Vicki: *Why would I be upset about Brian? I broke up with him. Katherine can have him.*

When you formulate the sentence to use for recovering from your broken relationship, approach the situation from many angles. If one tapping sentence doesn't work, switch to another, and another, until you come up with the right one. It's possible that you are feeling miserable because you've been rejected. But it's also possible you feel miserable because you are alone and you're afraid to be alone; or because you won't have a partner for a particular upcoming event, or because you feel you were made a fool of. Examine your situation from all angles and then tap on all angles and you will cure yourself. You don't necessarily have to say your full sentences on every tapping spot. Use your key word whenever you wish.

True Report

SHE WAS A beautiful woman and I loved her. She left me and I had a great desire to stalk her. Actually, I did for a while. My therapist was afraid I'd get arrested before the therapy would work, so she told me to see you for tapping. Now I'm still in therapy but I wonder why, because as soon as we tapped I didn't want her back. Actually, it wasn't so much tapping that did it for me, it was rubbing the Pledge spot.

—Boris

BEREAVED

Helen enjoyed a delightful marriage. She and Al had been best friends since college. Now that their children were grown, they had even more time to take pleasure in one another and to travel and play golf and entertain friends in their country house. It was a good life—and Al's sudden death from a heart attack shocked Helen. She did whatever needed to be done—attended to the children and grandchildren, consulted the lawyers and financial advisers—but she could not stop crying. She wept while she drove, she wept while she cooked. She cried herself to sleep at night and she awakened in the morning with her eyes full of tears. Her family doctor assured her it was normal to feel bereft and upset. She knew, too, that her behavior was predictable, but her heart ached and she begged for relief. The pain was too much.

Helen came to my office to try tapping. "All I ask is for one day of peace, so I can get my bearings," she pleaded.

We talked, and Helen came up with six sentences:

- *Even though I am all alone I'll be OK*
- *Even though Al is gone I'll be OK*
- *Even though I have to drive to the country by myself I'll be OK*
- *Even though I sit alone at the table I am OK*
- *Even though Al is not here to guide our family I am OK*
- *Even though I sleep alone in the big bed I am OK*

Helen's key words were *alone, gone, driving, eating, guiding,* and *bed.* She tapped on all the tapping spots for each sentence and each time she went from a D or an F right down to an A with just one, two, or three rounds of tapping. Yet, when she finished the last of the sentences, she said she was relieved with all we'd done but felt there was so much more to do. She said she still felt terrible.

I realized that I needed to function as a psychotherapist and bereavement counselor in order to help Helen. I suspected that there were negative feelings within her that she was reluctant to reveal.

Dr. Roberta: *What is it that makes you most upset? What thought do you have that makes you angry?*

Helen: *I can't believe he did this to me. He left me. He left me just when I retired and have time on my hands. He did this to me and I am mad at him, even if it was not his choice and even if my saying this is not rational. I am mad.*

So she tapped on: *Even though I am angry that Al left me I am OK.* Helen began as an F and after one round went down to a B. She said the Pinkie spot seemed most useful, so she tapped on that for about fifteen seconds. "Now I'm at an A," she announced, "but I am still upset about other things. I don't know what they are, though; I just feel upset inside me."

Dr. Roberta: *Don't worry about knowing what's upsetting you. That's my job. Try telling me what you are most afraid of today.*

Helen: *That's easy. I'm afraid I'm going to make a mistake with money. Al left me well provided for, but he used to spend time every day going over our stock portfolio. I don't know anything about the stock market. What if I lose all our money? He worked so hard to build all this. I could lose it in one fell swoop.*

Dr. Roberta: *Did Al have accountants and lawyers he trusted?*

Helen: *Yes, he did. I know them, too.*

Dr. Roberta: *You must call them and let them know where you stand. They will advise you. Don't worry. Do you feel that you were left with too big a burden?*

Helen: *Exactly.*

I suggested that Helen tap on: *Even though Al left me a big burden I am OK.*

(Key word: *burden.*) This seemed to do the trick. Helen was more relaxed and made an immediate plan to meet with her financial helpers.

Bereavement can be complex, and you must look at all angles of it. A relationship that lasts a lifetime will have had many facets to it, all of which will affect the grief-stricken person. You may have to identify all the facets and tap for each one.

If you are bereaved or otherwise suffering from the loss of a loved one, I suggest you tap on all your tapping spots and then tap on Eyebrow One, Under-Eye, Side, Pinkie, Collarbone, and V.

Pining for a lost love, with those painful feelings of longing, really hurts. Tapping will help.

Hot Spots

Bereavement responds well to the full sequence of tapping spots and to Eyebrow One, Under-Eye, Side, Pinkie, Collarbone, and V. Repeat this several times.

SAD?

JUST AS THE Tapping Cure cannot cure pneumonia, so it cannot cure depression. Pneumonia is a disease of the lungs and a major clinical depression is a disease of the brain. Both diseases require immediate medical attention.

That said, while your depression is being treated, tapping can help to lift your spirits a bit. Tapping is not a replacement for medical treatment, but it could be a quick fix to help your mood while you wait for the traditional treatment to do its job. It could also help eradicate a few of the thoughts that are so troublesome during an episode of depression.

Tapping on Eyebrow One helps with sadness, as does tapping on V. Consider tapping on the V spot for a full minute. Sometimes that does wonders. If you decide to do a full tap, on all tapping spots, an appropriate sentence might be: *Even though I feel so sad I am OK.*

You might want to add other sentences to cover all the negative feelings you are having. For example,

- *Even though I have crazy thoughts in my head I am OK*
- *Even though I don't want to go to work I am OK*
- *Even though I want to stay in bed all day I am OK*
- *Even though my mood sinks for no apparent reason I accept myself*
- *Even though I cannot control my feelings I accept myself*

Your key word might be *depression* or *sadness.*

Remember, depression is a treatable disease. When you get to the right mental health professional and are presented with the right treatment, you will feel much better. Tapping may alleviate some of your distress, but additional management is usually necessary, too.

TIRED?

ARE YOU TIRED and lacking motivation? Tap on your Karate spot. It often relieves fatigue and gets you going. While tapping, say: *Even though I am feeling lazy and tired I accept myself.*

If that doesn't do the trick, then tap on your V spot. Karate and V are tapping spots that help with motivation, as are Under-Eye and Collarbone. The V spot can perk you up. For a quick pick-me-up you may not need to tap all your spots; just one or two of these should work. Try them out and see which combination of the four works best for you. Of course, if you are tired because you are not getting enough sleep, please don't tap—just go to bed!

WISE WORDS

*In Charlotte's Web, by E. B. White,
Charlotte the spider advises Wilbur the pig:
"Never hurry and never worry."*

STRESSED OUT?

HERE'S A QUICK fix for a day when you are totally stressed and don't want to spend more than a minute tapping: Rub or tap both Eyebrow Two spots while you say: *Even though so much is going on around me I can stay calm and centered.* Take a deep breath and repeat the sentence while tapping both Collarbone spots. Then tap your Karate spot. That's all you need to do to regain your serenity.

Now that you know how to use the Tapping Cure to stay in control of your emotions, you will notice that there is less hassle and bother in your life. You are more and more joyful as you remain calm and comfortable in situations that used to cause you anguish. Please remember to tap. It works!

Remember This

You can change. You can enjoy your life. You can tap yourself to help facilitate change. Today is the first day of the rest of your life; start a new precedent. Accept yourself.

Trauma
and PTSD

REMEMBER HURRICANE KATRINA? Remember the tsunami? People who suffer through a natural disaster are at risk for becoming traumatized. Have you ever heard of shell shock? Of combat fatigue? These two terms were used during the last century to describe the condition of soldiers who had been exposed to horrifying wartime experiences. Today we would say those same soldiers, as well as disaster survivors, are suffering from PTSD.

WHO GETS PTSD?

WHILE PTSD CERTAINLY makes itself known after military combat, it also may occur in people who have experienced or witnessed:

- a natural disaster, such as a tsunami, an earthquake, or a hurricane;
- a terrorist incident, such as 9/11, a shooting, or a suicide bomber;

- a violent personal attack, such as a rape, a home invasion, or an assault;
- an accident, such as a car crash, a helicopter crash, or a sports melee.

Symptoms can also occur in people who've experienced difficult life situations that are not necessarily considered traumatic. Severe combat, death, and torture are not the only causes of symptoms of trauma. Sometimes events that are not life-threatening, such as job loss or divorce, can cause serious symptoms.

It's estimated that at some point in their lives 10 percent of women and 5 percent of men will experience PTSD. Women most often suffer from it after sexual abuse or physical abuse; men develop it after combat, childhood neglect, and sexual and physical abuse.

It wasn't until the Vietnam War that scientists and researchers began paying attention to the complaints of veterans who said they were suffering from memories of their wartime experiences. All wars that have been studied, in the United States and in other countries, seem to have produced veterans who experience similar symptoms, including difficulty sleeping, particularly because of nightmares; difficulty holding a job, particularly because of flashbacks; and a tendency toward disruptive relationships.

Please note that contrary to the so-called information you may pick up in the media, most people who are exposed to traumatic situations do not develop PTSD. Most people are resilient and resourceful. They may suffer for a bit, but then they get over it on their own, without outside help. The medically endorsed treatment for PTSD today is called exposure therapy and the results are good. However, I suggest you do not consider exposure therapy until you've tried to heal on your own. Time does have a healing effect, and exposure therapy is not as useful immediately after a trauma as it is after some time has elapsed. Many people are helped by tapping.

Try it, and if it doesn't work for you, don't continue to suffer. Find appropriate help.

DO YOU HAVE IT?

YOU KNOW YOU are suffering from PTSD if you experienced or witnessed a horrific event that caused you great fear as well as feelings of helplessness, and ever since that day you have suffered from certain symptoms, detailed in the list below.

- memories of the event intrude upon your mind during waking hours
- nightmares of the event disturb your sleep
- sometimes you feel that the experience is about to happen all over again
- you avoid any reminders of the event—activities, people, places, even conversation
- you feel isolated and separate from other people
- you're unable to show love to people to whom you used to be able to show love
- you're no longer interested in activities that you used to enjoy
- sometimes you cannot remember important parts of the traumatic incident
- you're on edge, irritable, and often angry
- you have difficulty concentrating
- you startle easily
- you notice that you are always on your guard

Remember, most people who are exposed to a traumatic, stressful event experience some of the above symptoms during the first few weeks after the event, and then their symptoms gradually go away. If you've developed PTSD, you will still have some of the symptoms listed above for many months—even years—after the trauma.

WHY DID YOU GET PTSD?

YOU ARE NOT crazy. You are not mentally ill. Most people who have psychiatric symptoms are suffering from an emotional disorder. But people who have PTSD are actually having normal reactions to an abnormal situation. It would be abnormal to continue with a jolly, happy life after experiencing a horrific event. But even though your reactions are appropriate, we do want you to get rid of them so that you can get on with your life and stop suffering.

Did you ever notice that when something really scary occurs it seems as if time stands still? If you've been in a car accident you may have felt, while the accident was occurring, that it was all happening in slow motion. Traumatic events totally overwhelm your regular coping mechanism and your brain actually experiences the trauma in a different way than it experiences regular events. During a trauma you are terrorized and you pay attention to only part of the experience; it is too much for you to absorb all that is going on. You may feel as if you are watching yourself in a movie.

The unusual way that horrifying events are experienced by your brain continues when your brain attempts to put the events into your memory. Instead of remembering the full experience, your brain admits only fragments of the experience. It is those fragments that come back to haunt you as flashbacks—images, sounds, smells, and feelings of the original experience. Trauma memories are stored differently in your brain. They are not stored as integrated experiences. That is why you do not get relief from traditional talk therapy. These traumatic memories are not responsive to reason.

GETTING RID OF PTSD

PSYCHOTHERAPISTS AND PSYCHIATRISTS are frustrated by the persistence of PTSD symptoms. Even with various therapies and medications and lots of effort, the success rate is small. A recent study showed that after 120 sessions of therapy, 75 percent of clients being treated for worrying too much after a trauma experienced *some* relief. That's right, 120 sessions! And they still had many symptoms. Much of the traditional treatment for PTSD is focused on managing flashbacks. Using the Tapping Cure, you can actually *eliminate* flashbacks.

There is evidence that the Tapping Cure can rapidly get rid of PTSD symptoms. So why isn't everyone using it? You know the reasons. There've been no scientific studies, and doctors in the United States are not quick to adopt unorthodox approaches. You don't have to take my word for the success of tapping away your trauma symptoms, even though I have interesting case studies to report. Let me tell you about the war victims in Kosovo.

KOSOVO

In 2000, a group of professionals who were trained in Thought Field Therapy, the tapping method developed by Dr. Roger Callahan, formed an organization to bring tapping to survivors of serious trauma throughout the world. The U.S. Agency for International Development, in Washington, D.C., asked the group to provide treatment to traumatized victims of war in Kosovo.

The group went to Kosovo on four separate occasions and treated a total of eighty-five trauma victims. On a typical day, they went to a village where hundreds of citizens had been herded into buildings and gunned down en masse. There they would work with the few survivors who'd escaped from beneath piles of dead bodies. Many had been tortured, many had starved, and most lost all family members. They suffered from many of the PTSD symptoms listed previously, and some also suffered from survivor's guilt.

Those who were treated ranged in age from four to seventy-eight, and they were evenly split between males and females. Tapping was a particularly useful therapy because not only was it effective, but it didn't require extensive language skills, so English-speaking health workers could easily treat Albanian patients. Translators came up with appropriate sentences and also explained the procedures, but there was no need for in-depth conversation and analysis. The patients and the practitioners were amazed by the results. Psychological distress was relieved immediately. The tapping team returned to Kosovo five months later to assess the situation, and sure enough, people were still cured; it was not a temporary fix.

Here are some excerpts from a letter written by Dr. Shkelzen Syla, chief of staff of the Medical Battalion of Kosovo Protection Corps, in Kosovo, to Dr. Callahan: "Many well-funded relief organizations have treated the post-traumatic stress here in Kosovo. . . . Kosovo had no real hope until volunteers came to us with your method. We referred our most difficult trauma patients. The success . . . was 100 percent for every patient, and they are still smiling until this day. As chief of staff of the Medical Battalion I have full authority over all medical decisions in Kosovo. I am starting a new national program. The emphasis of the national program will be Thought Field Therapy."

Despite such evidence of the effectiveness of tapping, the medical establishment is not convinced. Even though patients were relieved of symptoms, critics say that the study was not scientific enough. They believe there was not enough attention paid to the precise symptoms of each patient and the manner in which the tapping procedure was explained to them. Also, there were no control groups, so there is the possibility that these people might have gotten better over time, anyway.

While the trip to Kosovo was a success, it does not constitute a rigorous study. It is anecdotal and not scientific, and thus is not considered a model for official U.S. policy. Carl Johnson, a tapping practitioner who was a member of the Kosovo team, recently returned from Rwanda and the Democratic Republic of the Congo, where he worked with fifty citizens who had witnessed the deaths of family members. He said the follow-up contact asserted that almost all were maintaining their good emotional health. Johnson also worked with members of the Zulu Nation in South Africa. There, he tapped with ninety-seven people who had either witnessed their children dying of AIDS or the murder of family members, or were themselves tortured, assaulted, or otherwise terrorized. Again, his results were astounding. Again, there was no scientific study.

Therapist Monica Pignotti, a critic of the seat-of-the-pants way in which much of tapping work is conducted, has said that "properly designed controlled studies are the only way to get the establishment to sit up and take notice." Until that happens, the Carl Johnsons of the world, with all their altruism and skill, will certainly make a difference to the patients with whom they work, but not to the medical professionals who could benefit from learning this technique.

Wise Words

Although the world is very full of suffering,
it is also full of the overcoming of it.

—Helen Keller

MORE ANECDOTES

ANECDOTAL REPORTS ARE case-by-case descriptions of the treatment and its result. For your purpose, which is to get rid of your PTSD symptoms, anecdotal reports are just fine. You don't have to compare yourself to others, as in a clinical trial. You just have to get better.

Among my clients for whom tapping eliminated PTSD is Mike. Mike owns a parking lot in midtown Manhattan. One evening a customer came to retrieve his car and then stuck a gun into Mike's back. No one heard or saw anything. No one intervened. Mike complied with the robber's demands, but was shot anyway. He came to my office when he was well enough, physically, to return to work. But he was just too scared to get back into his routine. He tried it for a couple of days. He wanted to let his nephew, who was replacing him, go back to his own business. But Mike was so fearful on the days he worked that any time a black BMW pulled into the lot he had to use all his energy to fight the impulse to run. At home his sleep was disturbed and he had no appetite.

Mike's tapping sentence was *I am full of fear since the trauma.* He tapped on: *Even though I am full of fear since the trauma I am OK.* Mike could have used the word *robbery* or the word *mugging* rather than the word *trauma.* Most of my clients, unlike Mike, mention the specific horror that befell them.

Mike's report card grade remained at F no matter how much tapping he did. I suspected that the trauma to him was so great that he could not eradicate his symptoms all at once. So we talked about his situation and came up with two sentences to tap to: *Even though I am full of fear since the trauma I will be OK tomorrow* and *Even though I am full of fear since the trauma I will feel safe.*

Tapping on these, he went from an F to a B, and I thought that might be sufficient for one day's work. He made an appointment for the very next day. My plan was to offer the original sentence: *Even though I am full of fear since the trauma I am OK.*

However, Mike called and cancelled the appointment. He said he'd slept fine at night, awakened and eaten breakfast, and had felt like going in to work. He asked if he could come in later in the week. He called the morning of his appointment, saying, "Doc, I appreciate what you did for me. But I can't come in to see you. I'm too busy at work." That was good news. I called Mike about two years after his one appointment with me, for the purpose of verifying his results. He was too busy to say anything more than "Everything's good. Gotta run."

True Report

MY LIFE IS better since tapping. Tapping got me to relax. I used to be scared that someone in my new neighborhood would know me from the past. I was thinking that everybody who looked at me was about to attack me just like they really did when I was in prison. Nobody in my life now, except for my wife, knows that I once was in trouble with the law and had to go away. The thought of people knowing about my past was unbearable. But now I'm relaxed about it. It was a long time ago. I have a new life and a new family. If somebody does find out, it's not a big deal. I don't think about it anymore. And I don't think that every guy is about to whip out a razor.

—John

HIDDEN PTSD

SOMETIMES A PRESENTING symptom is caused by a trauma and is a manifestation of PTSD, but the trauma itself is not evident. That's what happened with Arthur, who is ten years old. His mother said that he had always been a sweet and cooperative child who'd had good relationships with his parents and brother. Suddenly, he started to rage at his brother and on two occasions beat him up for no obvious reason. Talking to Arthur offered no clue about his sudden change in behavior. We tapped on sentences about his brother and about his family life, but there was no progress. Recalling that his mother had said that it all began on April 1, I asked Arthur if he could remember April 1 and what he'd done that day. Bingo! That was the day that Arthur had been attacked by the school bully. His lunch money was taken and he was punched and smacked. Arthur happened to remember the date because he recalled initially saying to himself, maybe this is an April Fool's Day joke and this guy is just kidding. He never told his family about the attack. The rage within him was displaced onto his brother. Arthur quickly went from a D to an A by tapping on: *Even though I was attacked by Danny I am a good kid.*

Arthur did not want me to reveal his ordeal to his parents. Trauma survivors often need the distance provided by time before they are comfortable talking about the incidents that harmed them. Historians tell us that there are Holocaust survivors who did not speak about their experiences for decades. Psychologists tell us that there are sexual abuse survivors who do not disclose their experiences for many, many years. That's perfectly normal, and you should not be encouraged to speak about your suffering. It once was hypothesized that talking about your trauma would make your symptoms go away, but that theory has been disproved. If and when you are ready to speak about your trauma, you will do so. You won't need outside encouragement. When the time is right for you to explore your feelings, you will; until then it is your right to maintain silence. When keeping silent gets in the way of your life because thoughts and feelings are about to burst out of you, you will easily reveal your story to the appropriate person(s).

The Tapping Cure is a wise treatment because it does not force you to articulate that which is difficult to articulate. Instead, it respects your need to slowly process your experience at your own pace.

True Report

I TAP TO get rid of my childhood memories. I knew I'd be a better person if I wasn't haunted by those gruesome images every day. The tapping worked, but it did even more for me. It gave me energy that I never knew I had. I don't why this happened. Maybe it was energy that was being used to keep my memories hidden. Now I accomplish more in a day than I used to in a week. I never tapped since that day in your office. I hope I'm not supposed to, because I'm not sure about which spots to do. I'm OK now. Better than ever.

—Maria

WHAT ABOUT PSYCHOTHERAPY FOR PTSD?

THE TAPPING CURE can facilitate your return to your job or school and can get rid of many of your serious symptoms. However, it's a good idea to get some psychotherapy in addition to developing resilience. Resilient people are less likely to succumb to PTSD because they have learned how to speak soothingly to themselves, to find social support in their environment, and to free themselves from feelings of shame and guilt. These are the folks whose PTSD symptoms usually resolve by themselves in a couple of months.

The right therapist can help you make sense out of your horrific experience and also help you find ways to move on. If you feel hopeless about your future, it's a good idea to consult a psychotherapist. You will emerge from therapy with possibilities and plans for the days ahead.

Hot Spots

Trauma memories respond well to tapping on Eyebrow One, Collarbone, and V. Repeat several times, and your memory should be diminished or gone.

TREATING YOURSELF

IT'S TIME TO formulate a sentence to eliminate your trauma symptoms. Most traumas have many angles to them, so you might need many sentences. That's OK. Tapping on a sentence takes just a couple of minutes. You will eliminate the pain associated with each memory. The memory will exist, but it won't torment you; it will seem neutral. When you recall the traumatic event you will experience it with a sense of detachment.

Please begin by recalling the event. Make yourself as upset as you can tolerate, but don't make yourself sick with your memory. Try breaking up your trauma into small components. If you cannot tolerate recalling all the details of your traumatic experience, then just make yourself uncomfortable enough to get to a D or an F and then tap on: *Even though I have terrible memories of that day (name the day) I am OK* or *Even though I have terrible memories of that person (name the person) I am OK* or *Even though I have frightening thoughts about (name the experience) I am OK.*

Begin your healing now. Write your sentences, give yourself a key word, rate your level of emotional pain, and then start to tap. Begin with the Karate spot and then rub the Pledge spot, and then tap all your other spots. Keep tapping until you are down to an A. You'll be so relieved.

BEST TAPPING SPOTS

EVERY TRAUMA VICTIM with whom I've worked has said that Eyebrow One provided the most relief, and that the next most helpful spot was the Collarbone. People who were also very angry felt better after their Pinkie and Index spots were tapped. Sometimes tapping on the Mustache spot helps clients feel secure and safe enough to move on with their lives.

If you don't go all the way down to an A, try concentrating on Eyebrow One, Collarbone, and V. Do this sequence twice. If you still need more help, tap on Eyebrow One, Under-Eye, Side, Collarbone, and V.

Not quite there yet? Try rubbing your Pledge spot once again. And then go through the entire sequence of all tapping spots. Make your sentences as specific as you can. If there are elements of guilt or anger mixed in with your feelings about the trauma, then tap on your Pinkie and Index spots for thirty seconds each. Also keep in mind that sometimes people erroneously blame themselves in thinking that they should not have been at a particular place or they should have listened to warnings about a particular person. Please don't do that. Don't lose sight of the fact that you did nothing wrong. You were the victim.

RECOVERING

IF YOU'VE BEEN suffering from PTSD for a long while, your body and your mind might need some extra time to accept all your new healthy feelings. Perhaps a day or two may need to elapse before you'll get to an A, but you'll notice progress each time you tap. You may find that certain sentences will be fully A, but some other sentences on which you are tapping may come down from F to D to C to B to A one day at a time. Usually tapping for PTSD will require some extra work, in the form of extra sentences. Here are some helpful sentences; use whichever apply to your situation.

Say them after you tap your regular sentences:

- *Even though I'm not fully over this, I accept myself*
- *Even though I'm not over this, it is safe to give up my symptoms*
- *Even though I'm still thinking about the trauma I am OK*
- *Even though I'm still suffering I deserve to get finished with this*

When you get down to an A for all your sentences, test yourself. Allow yourself to think about the horrendous episode and notice that you can think of the incident while your emotions remain detached. Your suffering has ceased. You did this by yourself. Congratulations.

LETTING GO

IF YOU'VE BEEN suffering from the aftereffects of trauma for a long, long time, it may seem weird to no longer have any symptoms. If you devoted every day to trying to prevent certain memories from popping up, and if you devoted every night to trying to sleep without nightmares, you will now have an interesting dilemma. You'll need to figure out what to do with all the time you suddenly have on your hands. Yes, that's right. Obsessing and worrying take up time. You are now freed from debilitating thoughts and feelings. You have more time. You no longer need to respond to life from the perspective of a victim. You no longer need to chase away bad memories. You may allow yourself to think of these once painful memories and you will have no negative emotions associated with the thoughts.

Some people tap every day, several times a day, for the first week after their initial Tapping Cure. During the second week they tap three times a day—upon awakening, sometime during the day, and then again at bedtime. For the third week they tap just once each day—and usually they do not complete that third week, because the symptoms they used to have seem like they occurred so long ago, and their memory of them is so faint, that there is no reason to address them.

This is the time to find your way back to some of the activities that you enjoyed before the trauma. Find a new purpose, a new hobby, a new mission, or even a new faith. You no longer need to obsess about yourself. Your body and mind will take care of you without your vigilance. Now you can find something outside of yourself, something greater than yourself, to believe in, to work for, to enjoy. Good luck.

Remember This

DON'T MAKE YOURSELF sick when you recall traumatic events. Think about them enough to bring them into consciousness, but stop the thoughts before they upset you too much.

Fine-Tuning
Your Results

OR MOST PEOPLE, most of the time, tapping on the full sequence of spots eradicates a problem. For some people, some of the time, tapping on just a few spots eradicates a problem. Sometimes, though, the tapping works only somewhat. Or it works wonderfully well for a while, and then the problem reappears. This chapter will help you overcome hindrances to a permanent cure. You will learn how to modify, enhance, and totally personalize your Tapping Cure.

UP AND DOWN AND UP

SOME PEOPLE BEGIN at an F and tap themselves down to an A, but then go back up to a D or an F within a couple of minutes. Your Pledge spot is the best spot to use in this situation. Rub the spot while saying: *Even though I still have my symptoms I'm OK.*

SEALING IN YOUR GOOD RESULTS

TO ENSURE THAT you will stay at an A after you are finished tapping your sequence, tap on the V spot. While tapping, look straight ahead, then look down at the floor, then, without moving your head, look up toward the ceiling, and then resume a normal eye position. Remember to move only your eyes, not your head. This is an eye roll, which helps to make the Tapping Cure permanent.

If you've reached an A and you're nervous—perhaps you're thinking that maybe this won't last, it's too good to be true—please know that statistically the success you achieve will last. But if you want to be extra sure, then tap several times a day, every day, for a week. Tap first thing in the morning, tap after breakfast, lunch, and dinner, and then tap again at bedtime. Tap when you are in the shower and tap when you are in your car and stopped at a traffic light.

SPECIAL ADDITIONS

HERE ARE SOME tapping techniques to use when you want to add more power to your treatment. All of these methods have been tested on clients. Each suggested variation will appeal to some people, but not everyone. If you've chosen a technique that is right for you, you will feel the difference either immediately, or shortly after you finish tapping. You will then know that this is something you should add to your regular tapping routine. I suggest that you try each of these methods one at a time. That is, try one on Monday, a different one on Tuesday. And, of course, if one is successful, you'll never need to try any of the others.

- At least once a day, do the tapping in front of a mirror.
- Tap bilaterally. Use both hands and tap both Eyebrow One spots, both Eyebrow Two spots, both Collarbone spots, and both Under-Eye spots.
- Speed up your tapping. Rush from spot to spot.
- Slow down your tapping. Tap each spot in an unhurried, leisurely fashion.
- If you know that one spot is particularly effective for you, then tap that spot in between each of the other spots.

- Drink water before you begin and then after you finish your sequence. (Many practitioners of energy psychology believe that this is extremely important and insist that their clients regularly drink plenty of water.)
- Ask another person to tap on your spots for you.
- Vary the time of day and the room you are in when you tap.
- Instead of tapping, just press your spots.
- Instead of tapping, rub your spots.
- Don't tap when you are hungry. Eat first and then tap.
- When you say your sentence and key word, shout them out.
- When you say your sentence, sing it out.
- Jump up and down several times before you begin your tapping.
- As you tap each spot, inhale, then exhale, all the while thinking of your situation and saying the key word.
- Rub your Pledge spot while saying your sentence loudly, clearly, and as if you believe in it with all your heart. Do this several times during the day, not necessarily during a tapping routine.
- Does the V spot help you? Use it after every tapping sequence.
- If you're right-handed, use your left hand to tap; if you're left-handed, use your right hand for tapping.
- Try power-tapping—it's more like banging—but be careful and don't hurt yourself.
- Tap in silence. Do not say any sentence. Think about your goal while tapping.
- Roll your eyes up as far as they will go, and then back down, when you finish your tapping sequence. Tap on your V spot while rolling your eyes.
- Alternate saying your full sentence with saying only your key word.

True Report

MAYBE I'M AN exhibitionist or something. I love singing my sentences. Now my entire building, or at least the neighbors on my floor, know all about my love life. I tap whenever I miss Danny and sing for all the world to hear: *Even though Danny is out of my life I am a winner.*

—Lynette

STUCK AT *A B* OR *A C* ?

IF YOU CAN'T get down to an A, then tap on your Karate spot while saying:

- *Even though I want to hold on to this problem I accept myself*
- *Even though I deserve this problem I accept myself*
- *Even though I am scared to let go of this problem I accept myself*
- *Even though I'll feel bad without this problem I accept myself*
- *Even though it's not safe to get over this problem I accept myself*
- *Even though I still have some of this problem left I accept myself*

Try to assess your situation objectively and see if there is a reason why you might want to hold on to your symptom. An unconscious conflict might not make itself known to you, but you can tap it away, anyway. Simply say all of the sentences suggested above, and you will dissolve any unknown blocks to your success.

Still not at an A? This time tap your Chin spot while you say: *Even though I don't deserve to be over this problem I am OK.*

Still not at an A? Tap your Mustache spot while you say: *Even though I may never completely get rid of this problem I am OK* or *Even though I may never completely get rid of this problem I accept myself.*

Remarkably, after tapping and talking and doing all that I have advised you to do, you will be free of the painful negative emotions that had been bothering you.

True Report

I CAN'T BELIEVE how easy this is. I took your advice and tried many different spots. Now I tap only on two fingers. That's all. My symptoms are gone and I feel good. I can socialize and speak in public and never feel guilty about succeeding. I try my best and feel good, not bad, when I get compliments. When my boss praises me I say thank you; I used to think he was teasing or being sarcastic. I always have my fingers with me and no one can see when I am tapping them, so even though I don't need to tap anymore that is reassuring. I hope to meet you one day. Thank you.

—Cara

SENTENCE STRUCTURE

THE LAST PART of your sentence is usually either *I accept myself* or *I am OK*. But, occasionally, you will respond better to sentence endings such as:

- *I will get rid of these negative symptoms*
- *I know I'll soon be fine*
- *I deserve to feel good*
- *I am terrific*

Thus, a person who does not respond to *Even though I freak out when I see blood I am OK* may respond to *Even though I freak out when I see blood I am terrific*. Experiment until you come up with the perfect sentence for you.

VARIATIONS ON A THEME

IT IS SOMETIMES difficult to know all the angles of your situation. Many situations need more than one sentence. Concentrate on the circumstance for which you are tapping and try to uncover all the angles it contains. There can be many different slants to what seems like a simple issue. For example, Andrea came to my office because she was feeling terribly stressed from caring for her mother. Her mother was in an assisted-living facility. Andrea was the only one of her siblings who lived in the same town as their mother. Although Andrea had a husband and two children and a full-time job, she had been going to the home every evening. After dinner she slipped out of the cozy, comfortable suburban home she owned, drove for about fifteen minutes, went to her mother's bedside and remained there for thirty to forty minutes while her mother criticized her, berated her, and asked why her husband and children were not there, too. Andrea endured this and then went directly home to help with homework, put in a load of laundry, and prepare for the next day.

Andrea's presenting symptom to me was anger. She was angry at her mother for not appreciating what she went through to get to see her. Andrea used the key words *angry at Mom* and we tapped on: *Even though my mother thinks I am negligent I am OK.* Then we tried: *Even though my mother criticizes me I accept myself.*

After tapping, Andrea felt less angry, but within minutes the anger was back. She said she felt upset again. So, this time we talked. I took notes while she told me about her mother. Here's what Andrea said:

"It's so hard to do everything. My kids are busy with homework and with their lives. I can't count on them to help with dinner or cleanup. My husband is exhausted when he gets home from work. He has a long commute. My brother is starting a business in Connecticut. He's got his hands full. My sister lives about three hundred miles away. She can't visit Mom. I do the best I can and Mom is lonely and getting a little paranoid, too. She sometimes thinks I want to steal her things. She doesn't have anything that anybody would want to steal. I am upset and clenching my jaw and clenching my fists all day long. I never get a break. My friend told me that your Tapping Cure worked a miracle for her. How come it's not working for me? Please help. I can't go on like this. I'm shouting at my co-workers and shouting at my kids. I'm ignoring my husband. Something has to give and I don't want it to be me."

When Andrea finished speaking, I proceeded to read back my notes to her and instructed her to tap on all sentences that had emotional connotations. Almost every sentence she had uttered required tapping. We tapped on:

- *Even though it's so hard to do everything I am OK*
- *Even though my kids don't help me I am OK*
- *Even though my husband doesn't help me I am OK*
- *Even though my brother doesn't help me I am OK*
- *Even though my sister doesn't help me I am OK*
- *Even though Mom accuses me of things I haven't done I am OK*
- *Even though I never get a break I am OK*
- *Even though I am impatient I am OK*
- *Even though I want to be left alone I am OK*

Andrea tapped a full sequence, beginning with the Karate spot and the Pledge, for each sentence. You might think that's a lot of work, but actually it took less than two minutes for each sentence. After the first few sentences, she felt better. She said she didn't feel upset anymore and her report card grade was an A. Soon, though, when I asked her to think about visiting her mother, she went up to a C. That's when we added the rest of the sentences. Each sentence was necessary. Each sentence represented another angle of her situation. When you tap, please investigate all angles of your situation.

Interestingly, when Andrea tapped on the first few sentences she felt particularly comforted by the Under-Eye spot and the Collarbone spot. Both of those spots work well with anger and with irritability.

Later on in her list, Andrea said that the Pinkie spot immediately helped her. Pinkie often helps with rage. Also, Eyebrow Two helped Andrea when she tapped about impatience. Impatience responds well to Eyebrow Two.

Hot Spots

Your Eyebrow Two spot (or both Eyebrow Two spots) may be useful when you are suffering from frustration and impatience.

SURPRISING VARIATIONS

GARY CAME TO my office needing help adjusting to his new state, that of a divorced man. He had been married to Suzie for eight years when she admitted that she had fallen in love with her boss and asked for a divorce. Gary was stunned. He had had no clue about their affair. He was angry. He was depressed. And, most of all, he was overwhelmed. Single life had held no appeal to him years ago and it did not now. Gary needed all the help he could get. Instead of my usual quick fix, which begins with *Nice to meet you* and ends with *We'll never meet again,* it was necessary for me to schedule several appointments with Gary. He needed emotional support and he also needed to deal with the many angles of his situation. If I were not a trained and experienced psychotherapist, I would have referred him elsewhere while continuing to see him for occasional tapping sessions.

Our first session we tapped on: *Even though my wife betrayed me I am OK* and *Even though my wife wants a divorce I am OK.*

His key word was *wife* and he swiftly went from an F to an A. Predictably, two weeks later he returned and said he was a D when he thought about his wife leaving him.

That's when we tapped on: *Even though I am not good enough for my wife I am OK.* We talked a bit about his wife's thinking he was good enough to marry and then changing her mind after the fact. Gary felt somewhat relieved when he left the office and scheduled another tapping session for two weeks later.

When he walked in for his next appointment Gary said, "Now that I realize that my wife doesn't want me anymore, I can admit to myself that I don't really want her. I haven't liked her very much these past few years. In fact, if I met her today for the first time I would not be interested in pursuing a relationship with her."

The new and final angle he then tapped on was: *Even though I no longer love my wife I am OK.* Gary surprised himself and at this point acknowledged that the divorce was OK with him. He began to plan for his future.

COMPLICATED SITUATIONS

IF YOUR SITUATION is complex, identify all the aspects that pertain to it and tap for each one. Sometimes it helps to write out a list of all possible problems; at other times it may help to talk about your circumstance with a friend, a counselor, or a family member. The more information you dig up from your mind, the more precise your tapping will be, and the sooner you will be cured.

It won't be long before you'll be finished with your problem situation forever.

DR. CALLAHAN'S GAMUT

PSYCHOLOGIST ROGER CALLAHAN, the Thought Field Therapy guru, believes that everyone does better when including what he calls the 9 Gamut Step in their tapping sequence. In my experience, plenty of clients, in fact most, do just fine without it. However, in case you need additional help in reaching an A, here is my version of Dr. Callahan's Gamut treatment. Consider following this routine after each full tapping sequence is completed and then tap the full sequence again.

- Tap on your V spot. You will continue tapping and complete the remaining steps while tapping on your V spot.
- Next you will close your eyes for a few seconds. Then open your eyes.
- Keeping your head motionless, look down at the floor opposite you, to the right.
- Next, shift your gaze and look down at the floor opposite you to the left. You are still tapping your V spot.
- Now pretend there is a clock facing you. Look at the number twelve on the imaginary clock. Whirl your eyes around in a circle, all the way past numbers one, two, and three, all the way to the number eleven and then twelve. Good.
- Next, go backward around the imaginary clock. Begin at twelve, whirl your eyes back past numbers eleven, ten, and nine, all the way around to number one and then twelve again.
- Next hum a tune for a few seconds. Try a bit of "Happy Birthday" or "Yankee Doodle" or your favorite popular song. No need to hum for more than five seconds. Remember, you are still tapping your V Spot.
- After humming, recite the days of the week.
- Now hum your tune once again for a few seconds.

You've completed your nine steps; resume your regular tapping sequence and you should easily reach your goal of an A when you ask yourself to rate your degree of upset. In other words, you are no longer upset when you think of that very incident that upset you so much just a short time ago. You now have no emotional response when you think of that original situation. In fact, you may wonder why in the world it bothered you in the first place.

*When you are a Bear of Very Little Brain,
and you Think of Things, you find sometimes that a
Thing which seemed very Thingish inside you is
quite different when it gets out into the open and
has other people looking at it.*

—A. A. Milne, in Winnie the Pooh

MORE SENTENCES

WORDING IS IMPORTANT. You can fine-tune your tapping session by being fussy about the words you choose for your sentence. Here is a list of some sentences that are useful; one may be appropriate for you:

- *Even though I am very upset about _____ I accept myself.*
- *Even though I feel so bad about _____ I'm getting over it.*
- *Even though I did something really stupid I am OK.*
- *Even though I did something really stupid I forgive myself.*
- *Even though I will have to bear the responsibility and punishment for what I did I am OK.*
- *Even though I'm a mess now I accept myself.*
- *Even though I used to think _____ now I know the truth.*
- *Even though I'm a mess now, soon this will be just a vague memory.*
- *Even though _____ happened it's no longer important to me.*

DOUBLE-CHECKING

WHEN YOU'VE SUCCESSFULLY tapped and happily reached your goal, you know that you can think of a once-painful circumstance and not be bothered. You'll have the thought and/or the memory, but you'll think it's not a big deal. You may even wonder why you used to spend so much time being upset about that situation.

True Report

I WISH I could do college all over again. For my five years there— yes, it took me extra long—all I did was think about my uncle and the way he molested me for so many years. My thoughts about the past and being sexually abused took the joy out of me. Now weeks go by when I don't even think about it. If it does cross my mind, it doesn't destroy me like it used to. I know he's a sicko and I know he's been punished. My best thought now is the magic of Eyebrow Two, Under-Eye, Side, and Collarbone. I do that tap routine once, then do the 9 Gamut, and then the routine again. These days I only have to do it about once a month, and that's only when I'm going to see my cousins.

—Donna

To make sure you remain free of negative feelings, it's a good idea to examine all aspects related to the situation. Think about it from every angle. The tapping should have eradicated all traces of feelings. The connection between the event and your emotional response has been broken. You are responsible for your wonderful cure. You have tapped, and tapping rewires the connections in your brain and creates a fundamental mind shift. This shift actually shatters the original connection between your thought and your feelings.

In your mind, bring up your thoughts about every part of the situation and for each part, each angle, check to be certain you have no residual emotion. If there's any hint of feeling, just tap on that angle. Don't be afraid of testing and checking. Double-checking strengthens any residual weakness by encouraging extra tapping on just the right angle.

My client Harry is an elderly man who had recently had some serious medical complications. Harry's doctor thought it was time for Harry to move beyond his fixation on his body. Harry, though, was still worried about his health and would call the doctor's office several times each day. He reported minor complaints as well as observations about his breathing, his walking, his appetite, his digestion, and his sleep patterns. Harry's doctor referred him to me for traditional psychotherapy. I had other ideas:

Harry: *You know, I lived all these years and never needed a shrink. I don't see why I need one now.*

Dr. Roberta: *You are right. Let's not shrink you. Instead, let's figure out what it is that's making you so nervous about your health.*

Harry: *Are you kidding? Three weeks in the hospital would make anybody nervous.*

Dr. Roberta: *That's true, but now that you've been discharged for six weeks you can be less vigilant. You can start to get back to regular.*

Harry: *I can't do that. My body acted up on me once and it could do it again.*

Dr. Roberta: *I have a plan. Let's identify the warning signals that you and your doctor agree would be serious signs. Then, any days that you don't have those symptoms you can enjoy yourself and not be nervous. Will you agree to my plan?*

Harry agreed. We contacted his internist and a few days later I was provided with a list of danger signals. Harry came back to my office and we went over the list. It specified the conditions that should prompt a call for help. It was a fairly extensive list and that pleased Harry.

Harry: *This is a big list, but I do think days go by when none of these things happen to me.*

Dr. Roberta: *Would you like to be able to stop worrying on those days? Would you like to spend those days having a regular life without panic about medical possibilities?*

Harry: *Yeah, it would be good. But it's impossible for me to get this medical stuff out of my head.*

I introduced the tapping concept and the idea that situations have many angles. We talked and came up with the following sentences:

- *Even though my body betrayed me I'm OK*
- *Even though I am not in total control I am OK*
- *Even though I had to be dependent upon my son and his new wife I am OK*
- *Even though the hospital atmosphere is like poison I am OK*
- *Even though my doctor doesn't return calls promptly I can deal with that*
- *Even though I may never be like I used to be I am OK.*

The spots that worked best for Harry were: Pinkie, Collarbone, Side, and then the 9 Gamut, and then a repeat of Pinkie, Collarbone, Side.

Harry said that while tapping his pinkie he felt the anger slipping out of him and while tapping his collarbone he felt his anxiety diminishing. I think most of all Harry was glad he didn't have to go through a long psychotherapy process. We took care of his symptoms in two sessions.

NO RESULTS?

YOU CAN CHANGE your tapping spots and the way you tap them. Your body and your mind are unique and your tapping experience will reflect that uniqueness.

Hot Spots

Tapping with both hands on Eyebrow One, Eyebrow Two, Under-Eye, and Collarbone can make a big difference. Consider tapping on both Side spots simultaneously, too. Do this by tapping with your thumbs or by crossing your arms in front of you.

Keep in mind that the suggestions in this book are a guide and not necessarily an exact formula. The Tapping Cure works for almost everyone. But every once in a while I come across someone for whom tapping does not work. Just as some people do not respond to particular antibiotics and other folks may have surgery that doesn't cure them, so there are people for whom tapping is not the treatment of choice. If you are one of those people, please go to a conventional mental health practitioner for treatment. Consult with as many doctors as possible until you feel better. You deserve to be symptom-free and sooner or later you will be. If tapping is the first treatment you tried, you are lucky because you invested very little time, you paid no great fees, and you took no medicines. Do keep in mind that one size fits most, not all. So don't be foolish and don't stick with tapping if you are not getting better.

Remember This

THERE ARE MANY variations to tapping. Probably one is just right for you. Experiment with all the possible enhancements, and in particular try the eye roll and the 9 Gamut. And do drink plenty of water.

Tapping for
Children and Babies

I'M A TYPICAL parent in that I can only be as happy as my most unhappy child. When one of my children—or grandchildren—is suffering, I, too, suffer. I want so much for their suffering to stop. If you are a parent, you know that feeling, and you know how often you've wished for magic. If you are a pediatrician or a pediatric nurse, you know how often you, too, have wished for magic. Well, you'll be pleased to know that tapping works indeed like magic with babies and with children! Whether you live with kids or work with kids, you'll benefit from learning these kids' tapping techniques. Not only will you be delighted because the results are quick, you'll be delighted because the price is right and because you'll effect a change in the child without medication.

KNOW THE CAUSE

BEFORE YOU BEGIN tapping on a baby or small child, one who cannot yet speak, you should know why they are miserable. Don't tap to quiet a crying baby until you know why it is crying. Tapping will get the baby to stop the tears, but what if the tears were caused by an ear infection that needs medication? Or a strep throat that needs antibiotics? Check with a doctor first. Don't tap until you know why the baby is crying.

If you know your toddler is screaming because he just fell and skinned his knee and you've already attended to the scrape, you can then tap away his pain in seconds.

Here's what you do: Hold the baby on your lap and gently, with love, tap his Karate spot. Say some soothing words while tapping for about ten seconds. Simply repeating *I love you* or *there, there* or some lines from a lullaby should do the trick. If the crying begins again, tap again. Perhaps you'll need to do several ten-second taps. Babies need to be tapped with only one finger, although sometimes two fingers may be most comfortable for you, and that's just fine. For most babies, most of the time, in less than one minute there is total contentment.

BABY TAPPING

MOST BABIES RESPOND swiftly to Karate spot tapping. I've seen babies stop crying in mid-sob when the tapping begins. In an informal experiment in a day care center in New Jersey, I observed one group of nannies lift crying babies to their laps and speak soothingly to them, while other nannies lifted their babies, soothed them with words, and also tapped their Karate spots. The latter group all stopped crying. The former group, offered comfort but no taps, did include several babies who slowed down their crying, but some continued crying and only one totally stopped.

In another, similar situation, parents who tried tapping on their extremely irritable babies got good results. The babies were in cribs or bassinets, and most of them quickly calmed down when they were tapped on the Karate spot and/or the Collarbone spot. The experimental conditions described above do not meet the stringent criteria of our government health organizations, so the good results will not be announced to all child-care workers and pediatric health professionals. But you now know the magic and you can begin spreading it around. When you lift a crying tot, simply start tapping and see what happens. You will be amazed.

Baby taps must be gentle taps, and your tone must be calm. It's possible that light touching on the tapping spots is all that is necessary, and actual tapping may not always be required. Some parents as well as some pediatric nurses have reported that rubbing gently on tapping spots has worked well, too. Sitting in your lap, your baby or toddler will quickly respond and you will experience great relief knowing there is something that you can do to comfort your anguished child. Babies respond to baby-whisperers—loving people who quietly soothe and comfort.

True Report

ON ONE OF those hot days last summer Julia was cranky and crying while we were at our swim club. I know I shouldn't have been embarrassed, but I was. I was thinking that all the other families had well-behaved children and I was probably getting a reputation as an incompetent mother. In desperation I remembered what you taught me and put Julia on my lap and spoke to her and tapped her. I spoke in a repetitive rhythm, like you suggested, and I tapped her collarbone, her side, and her hand. I lightly tapped her Karate spot and her V Spot on her hand. I went back and forth from one to the other. She didn't cry for the rest of the day and I felt so much better about myself that I could relax and enjoy the day, too.

—Carol

TALKING TO BABY

ALTHOUGH LANGUAGE IS not yet understood by these little ones, emotion is easily transmitted. Your love and caring will be picked up by the baby's unconscious mind and will contribute to the healing process. Many practitioners of meridian psychotherapy believe that you should speak about the issues at hand, even to babies. According to their beliefs, your words should address the baby's probable feelings in a general way. So when you tap or rub your baby's tapping spots you might say:

- *Even though you are cranky you are a lovely little baby*
- *Even though you cry whenever you are in the car you are a sweet baby*
- *Even though you hate your crib you are a honey bunch*
- *Even though you are overtired and screaming you are a good baby*

Experiment with all of your baby's tapping spots and see if you agree that most infants and toddlers need only the Karate spot and their collarbones to be tapped, and some don't even need their collarbones; the Karate spot does it all.

ᴡᴏ WISE WORDS

A torn jacket is soon mended,
but hard words bruise the heart of a child.

—Henry Wadsworth Longfellow

TRY TAPPING YOURSELF, TOO

ON THE DAYS when you are frustrated and having a difficult time parenting an impossible child, you may be tempted to shout, "Shut up or I'll smack you." Instead, cure your exasperation by tapping yourself. Calm down by tapping on:

- *Even though my toddler has been saying "no" for two hours I am OK*

- *Even though I don't know how to get my baby to sleep I am OK*
- *Even though I haven't had a minute to myself in three weeks I am OK*
- *Even though my two-year-old threw many temper tantrums today I am OK*

When tapping, please remember that you, too, deserve to be tapped with love. The tapping spots that many people find particularly effective for reducing stress are Under-Eye, Side, and Collarbone. Try various combinations of these three and then add any other spots that work for you.

THE TAT POSE

IN THE 1990s, Tapas Fleming, an acupuncturist in California, experimented with touching various meridian spots on her patients without using her acupuncture needles. She developed a method of relieving traumatic stress and other emotional stress, even allergies, by using precise words while touching particular spots on the face and neck. For babies and young children this method, called TAT, for Tapas Acupressure Technique, is an effective calming method. I suggest you try it on your baby without necessarily saying the TAT words. Simply use your own sentences of comfort and kindness while holding your baby's head in the TAT pose.

The TAT pose is as follows: With your baby in your lap, place one hand on the back of your baby's head. Your thumb will be at the base of the hairline, your pinkie finger midway up the scalp. You are making a cradle for the head. With your other hand, gently place your palm over the top half of the baby's eyes and forehead. That's it. Now, using your own soothing words, speak to your child. You could begin your sentences with "Even though" and end with "I love you so much." For example: *Even though you are crying I love you so much;* or *Even though you are hurting I love you so much.* Or just say the words you usually do when you cheer up your child.

If you are curious about how this feels, put one hand behind your head, as described above, and place your other hand, palm down, over the top half of your eyes. Note that your hand is near the Eyebrow One and Eyebrow Two tapping spots. Cup your hand, and, using two fingers, perhaps your thumb and ring finger, touch the inner edges of both eyebrows. Then, with the two fingers in between, press on the center of your forehead, a bit above the nose. It is not recommended that you do this adult version with a baby because it is more intense and may be overwhelming. Maintain this pose while you speak to yourself. Say a meaningful phrase that will help you cope with whatever situation is disturbing you. If this works for you, you'll notice immediate results.

Fleming's research suggests that with both hands in the proper pose while the right words are being uttered, significant calming and healing occurs. Try it on yourself and your baby and your older child, too. This is an opportunity for you to learn yet another energy psychology technique based upon meridian therapy.

THE CHILD WHO WALKS AND TALKS

OLDER CHILDREN ARE fun to tap because they like the instant results. Also, rather than being embarrassed about tapping in public, as some adults are, children enjoy showing off their new tapping skills to anyone who will look and listen.

Younger children most often are tapped for separation anxiety and for fear of the dark. Older children may need tapping for test anxiety, for sports performance anxiety, and for bully-proofing. And of course all children who have been exposed to trauma need tapping to shed the emotional pain of their ordeal.

Children, like babies, may not need to use all their tapping spots. Most kids do well with just the Karate and V spots. I do find, though, that for some unknown reason girls are also helped by the Collarbone spot. And I've noticed—and it's also been reported to me by others—that when children are being tapped for issues having to do with other children, their finger spots are the most useful. Of course, you can always suggest that the children with whom you are working tap on all of the spots.

Most kids will prefer tapping themselves, but some younger ones will want you to tap them first to show them precisely where to do it. Some of the less mature kids like the idea of sitting in their parents' lap to be tapped. It is one of the few times when they are not ridiculed for wanting to act like a baby, and they're actually encouraged to sit in Mom or Dad's lap.

Hot Spots

Often babies and children are calmed when they're tapped on the Karate spot and/or V spot. You don't necessarily have to say a sentence—sometimes humming or singing works.

TEACHING YOUR CHILD TO TAP

YOUR CHILD MAY already be curious about tapping from watching you tap on yourself. That's a good thing. Your child also may be interested in knowing which are the best tapping spots on his or her body, and will be pleased to learn that you don't have that answer. It is his or her task to figure out the best tapping spots.

IDENTIFYING THE PROBLEM

If your son comes home from school grouchy and irritable, you know he's had a bad day. You ask what's wrong and he tells you about a teacher who's not fair, a kid who picks on him, and an embarrassing moment during gym. This is your opportunity to mention that you know a new method that can magically make his sadness about these incidents disappear. When his interest is piqued, I suggest you take out pencil and paper to record his answers to the questions you'll then ask. You already know there will be at least three angles to tap for—the teacher, the bully, and the gym class—that contributed to his bad day. For each angle you'll ask him to tell you about the incident in as much detail as possible and then write down the details to later help you formulate the best sentences. For each angle you'll want to know:

- What was the worst part of what happened?
- What was the most upsetting part of what happened?
- Did this remind you of something similar that once happened to you?
- Did you ever feel like this before? When?
- Who said what to whom?

The more you know, the more sentences you'll create to tap on, and the more likely your son will benefit from the Tapping Cure and be totally over the upset. As an added bonus, he will also be building resilience for coping with future incidents.

MEASURING DISTRESS

Once you've identified the problem(s), it's time to measure your child's level of unhappiness. It's not a good idea for children to use the grading system that adults use when figuring out how upset they are. Kids have enough trouble worrying about getting an F or obsessing about getting an A, so we should not be adding to their anxieties. Yet it's a good idea to know how distressed they are so that you know when to stop tapping, and when to change tapping spots and sentences.

In my office, to help children indicate their level of upset, I have a large carton filled with different-sized balls. There's a cotton ball, a Ping-Pong ball, a tennis ball, a soccer ball, and a large red beach ball. I ask the child to indicate the size of his unhappiness about the situation in question by choosing a corresponding ball. I might ask, "How scared are you? As much as this big beach ball?" And then I inform the child that we will tap until the unhappiness is as small as the cotton ball, or even smaller; perhaps so small that we can no longer see it without a magnifying glass.

Another good ideas is to draw a series of faces on separate sheets of paper—construction paper and heavy-weight paper work well. You might have several faces showing a progression of stages from unhappiness to happiness, where the mouth gradually goes from totally frowning to totally smiling. Three or four faces should be sufficient. Your goal is for the child to reach a perfect smiley face. Be creative and you'll come up with a good way to assess the child's progress.

Patricia French Crilly, RN, recommends that you refer to your child's problem as a *bother*. Crilly says, "This eliminates the need to ask negatively charged questions such as, 'What's your problem?' or 'What is wrong with you?' It's gentler and less threatening to ask a child, 'What's bothering you?'"

For children approximately seven to ten years old I sometimes use my *stand on chair* technique to assess their distress level. I'll ask the child to indicate how upset he/she is feeling by first watching me demonstrate different heights between floor and ceiling. I'll stand on my toes, reach up as high as possible, and say, "This is a very, very large amount of worry and disturbance." Then I'll bend close to the floor, put my hand out parallel to it and just a couple of inches above it, and say, "This is a very, very small amount of worry and disturbance." I'll ask the child to demonstrate how much the situation they've come to work on disturbs them. I allow them to stand on an old, sturdy chair that I drag into my office just for this purpose. The children enjoy this as an activity, feel empowered by it, and eagerly tap in order to be able to assess and demonstrate their new worry position.

FORMING YOUR SENTENCES

Begin by agreeing on a couple of sentence endings. Work with your child to come up with acceptable phrases that he or she will feel comfortable saying aloud. Some sentence endings for kids that usually work well are:

- *I love myself*
- *I'm a good kid*
- *I am lovable*
- *I'm pretty terrific*
- *I'm a wonderful girl/boy*
- *I'm a good person*
- *I like who I am*
- *I'm a winner*

Practice saying these sentences with your child.

Now return to your pencil and paper and, choosing one aspect of the problem, perhaps the unfair teacher, begin forming statements. You and your child might come up with:

- *Mr. Randall said I was cheating and I wasn't*
- *Mr. Randall never calls on me*
- *Mr. Randall has favorites and I'm not one of them*
- *Mr. Randall broke his promise about no homework*

Have these sentences on paper where your child can easily read them. Add *Even though* to the beginning of each sentence. Good. Now ask your child to choose an appropriate ending from the list of sentence endings you created.

Now you should have several sentences ready to be tapped on for this angle of your son's unhappiness in school. A typical sentence might be: *Even though Mr. Randall never calls on me I'm a good kid.*

KEY WORD

Ask your child to think of one or two words that will remind him or her of each sentence so he/she won't have to say all those words all the time. Perhaps *ignores me* would work for the above sentence.

WHO DOES THE TAPPING?

Nine-year-old Zachary came to my office with his mom to get help for his inability to fall asleep at night. Coincidentally, that very same day, Joseph, age eight, and his mom had an appointment for help with the same problem. Interestingly, Joseph chose to tap on himself while Zach wanted his mom to do the tapping. They both responded well to Under-Eye, Side, and Collarbone. Their sentence was: *Even though I have trouble falling asleep I am a superstar.* Follow-up reports from both moms indicated that Joseph was now falling asleep easily and quickly; Zachary needed his mom to tap him every night and then would promptly get to sleep. Children usually know whether they are comfortable being tapped by a parent or whether they prefer to do it themselves. I suspect their preference has more to do with their personality than with their age.

LEARNING TAPPING SPOTS

Ask your son to again indicate his level of distress. Then, go through the full sequence of tapping spots on your body and ask your son to follow along on his body, while thinking of how upset he is about the incident. Speak along with him. For the Karate spot and the Pledge spot you'll say the entire sentence. For the other spots you'll say the key words. After a full sequence, again ask your son to indicate his level of distress. Probably he'll be feeling much better. Do the tapping on all angles. Tap on every bit of discomfort he has experienced.

Together with your child, you will discover the best tapping spots for him. Remember that children usually need to tap on several, if not all, of their finger spots when their issues involve other kids.

True Report

WHEN I BROUGHT my son in for tapping, my husband thought I had lost my marbles and my pediatrician threatened to remove me from her case list. Josh had been suffering for too long and had seen too many shrinks with no improvement. We met Dr. Roberta and she explained the Tapping Cure. Josh has not missed one day of school since then, he has had no detention since then, and he is not bouncing off the wall when he comes home. He's actually a nice kid, like I always knew he was underneath everything. Josh taps now in school and says his sentence to himself. His sentence is: *Even though I am really very, very mad and even though nobody listens to me I am a good kid and everybody should listen to me.* This has made all the difference in my son.

—Cynthia

THE SHY CHILD

Occasionally a child is too shy to be tapped by me or by a parent, and may not want to cooperate at all. It's in anticipation of these circumstances that I ask parents to bring not only their child to my office but to also bring the child's favorite stuffed animal or doll. If your child is reluctant to tap when you are trying to get him/her to go through a tapping sequence, simply request that he or she go get a doll or stuffed animal. Begin the tapping on the doll. You tap the doll and then your child will probably want to tap, too. Sooner or later the transition will be made and your child will tap him- or herself or permit you to tap him/her when you say it is time to switch and tap on the child.

THE NONCOMMUNICATIVE CHILD

Fortunately for children who prefer to keep their struggles to themselves, the Tapping Cure can be successful without any information being revealed. Kids who want their privacy will feel much better after tapping on: *Even though this terrible thing happened I am OK* or *Even though a very bad thing occurred today I am OK* or *Even though the worst thing possible has happened I am OK.*

Many years ago a youngster appeared in my office. He had no appointment and he was not with a parent. He said he had heard about me from a neighbor who was a psychotherapy patient of mine, found my address in the telephone directory, and set out to find me. He told me his name was Robert and he asked about the cost for a session. When I told him, he counted out coins and singles from his pocket and said he could afford to pay half my fee. I was intrigued but knew I had legal constraints and could not treat a minor without parental consent; nor did I want to take his apparently hard-earned life savings. He was crestfallen when I began to explain that I could not begin a course of psychotherapy for him without his parents' permission. He looked so disappointed that I perhaps risked some liability by saying that I could help him anyway, for a fee of one dollar.

I explained that while I could not be his therapist, I could be his tapping coach; and while I would not be asking him to recount what must be desperate circumstances, his worries would disappear anyway. He was puzzled but trusted me. I showed him the tapping spots and asked him to fill in the blanks of the following sentence, without telling me anything more: *Even though _____ happened I'm a good kid and I'm OK and I respect myself.* Robert said he felt better after about three rounds of tapping the entire sequence. He paid me the dollar and left.

I thought about Robert every so often over the next few years and hoped he was OK. One day, on an early morning, my appointment book indicated that a gentleman named Bob had the first appointment of the day. When Bob entered the office his first words were, "I'm now over eighteen years of age. Will you treat me?" It took me a while to remember who he was, but, yes, it was Robert of long ago. I was so curious. What was that teenage appointment all about? Did he have a terrible life? A mysterious family? I was delighted; finally, I thought, I'll learn what really happened during that session. Alas, that was not to be.

Bob: *I have another issue. Can you help me figure out my tapping spots? I already know my tapping phrase.*

Dr. Roberta: *Oh? What is your sentence?*

Bob: *It's almost the same one I used last time. I use it every now and then when things crop up:* Even though blank happened I'm OK and I respect myself.

Dr. Roberta: *Now that you're an adult you might want to talk about some of these issues. You can, you know.*

Bob: *It's not my style. I'll stick with what worked before. I just wanted a little guidance about the tapping spots, that's all. I know that I'm a good tapper.*

And so we tapped. During the tapping Bob yawned a lot, a sure sign that something significant was going on. He left and that was that; or so I assumed.

A few months later Bob contacted me to say that he was very grateful for our last session. He said he was the only one in his family to tap and the only one in his family to come out intact after "the traumas." To this date I have no clue what went on in his family, but I do know that a noncommunicative adolescent grew to be a noncommunicative adult, and that's OK.

The Tapping Cure does not require talk therapy.

VARIATIONS

TAPPING ON CHILDREN, or having them tap on themselves, works well. Sometimes, though, kids get bored. Here are some variations should that occur:

- Don't tap. Instead, touch the spot and keep your fingers there while instructing the child to inhale through the nose and then exhale through the mouth. After each exhalation move on to the next spot.
- Don't tap. Instead, gently rub.
- Use stuffed animals and dolls to gain the child's interest.
- Alternate between tapping the child and having him/her tap him- or herself.
- Use the Tapas pose, described above. Depending upon the child's age, use either the baby version or the adult version.

CHILDREN'S ISSUES

MY TAPPING PRACTICE is probably typical. Kids are bothered by situations that are not all that unusual. Here are some sentences that kids, or their parents, chose to use in my office recently:

- *Even though I don't like to share I'm a good kid*
- *Even though I really want to kick Gerald I'm OK*
- *Even though I feel sad I'm a good person*
- *Even though I don't like to play at recess I'm OK*
- *Even though I'm afraid of the school bus I'm Mr. Wonderful*

If the parents are the ones to do all the tapping and all the talking, they would change the above to:

- *Even though you don't like to share you are still a good kid*
- *Even though you really want to kick Gerald you are still OK*

- *Even though you feel sad you are a good person*
- *Even though you don't like to play at recess you are OK*
- *Even though you are afraid of the school bus you are Mr. Wonderful*

Children have plenty of angles to their dilemmas. Take Darren. Tapping may take away Darren's urge to kick Gerald, but he may then want to punch Gerald. Darren needed to talk it out and eventually tap on the deepest layer of the problem. Problems do get peeled away with tapping. The immediate goal was accomplished when Darren was no longer getting into trouble at school for attempting to kick Gerald. But Darren's parents called me a couple of weeks later to report that their son seemed unhappy and was fussing about going to school in the morning. Last year, in kindergarten, he loved going to school. Talking it over in my office, it became clear that Gerald—the boy he wanted to kick—is very bright and catches on to new material quickly, while Darren is slower to learn. Darren is envious of Gerald's ability to win the teacher's praise. When we tapped on: *Even though I'm not the smartest boy in first grade I'm OK*, Darren's symptoms subsided, he settled down in school and at home, and the latest report from his dad was that he was doing very well as far as catching on to new work.

TEENAGERS' ISSUES

ADOLESCENTS CAN USUALLY follow an adult protocol when it comes to tapping, but sometimes they need some extra guidance. They can be so grown-up one moment and so childish the next; that is why parents, teachers, and therapists often complain about teens' erratic behavior.

LINDSAY

Teens are particularly concerned with their appearance, and that's why Lindsay wound up in my office. She's a pretty and poised high school student, so I was surprised when she said she was embarrassed by her looks. When I asked her to get specific, she showed me her hands. Lindsay was a nail biter and her fingertips were, indeed, "gross." I usually recommend one session of hypnosis to cure nail biting, but Lindsay insisted she wanted to try tapping instead. This required a few sentences:

- *Even though I bite my nails I am OK*
- *Even though I want to bite my nails I am OK*
- *Even though my fingertips are messed up they'll soon be OK*

Lindsay rated herself as extremely upset whenever she thought about the fact that she was a nail biter and whenever she looked at her nails. She tapped on the full sequence of tapping spots and then went back to tap on Mustache and Chin a few extra times. She left the office saying that she was no longer "too upset," and could more easily tolerate looking at her fingers. A few days later, Lindsay e-mailed me to let me know that she had stopped biting her nails "for no apparent reason." I followed up in a couple of months and Lindsay called herself "an ex–nail biter."

MATT

Matt is a teen who hoped I could help him tolerate parents, teachers, and "everybody else who is always on my case." He came to me as a last resort. He was getting into arguments with most of the adults in his life. I asked him if he wanted to be more cooperative and he said, "No, they are always telling me what to do. I'd rather do things my way." I suggested that his life would be a bit easier if he picked his fights and made an issue only out of the really important situations. We talked about this and finally Matt agreed that he would allow himself only one argument a day, and would acquiesce to all other "suggestions" once he had had his one fight.

This is an agreement that usually works well for rebellious teens because it gives them practice at being successful using self-control. Eventually their ability to tolerate "suggestions" becomes a habit.

I told Matt I could give him a secret weapon that would help him endure criticism and put up with interfering adults. The secret weapon would be a tapping technique. He was to tap his Karate spot and rub his Pledge spot anytime he felt hassled. He was to do this in such a way that no one else would notice. And, if he felt like it, he could say to himself, while tapping and rubbing: *Even though they are hassling me, I can stay calm.*

He practiced concealed tapping and disguised rubbing, and left the office feeling confident. His mom e-mailed me a few weeks later to report that Matt still told her nothing, but that she'd had no more calls from school authorities and far fewer fights in the family, so apparently the treatment was a success.

DONALD

Dr. Rita Seiden, a psychotherapist in Brooklyn, New York, told me about Donald, a seventeen-year-old high school student who was shy and came to her for help because he was terribly afraid of being called upon to speak aloud in class. He was afraid that he would stutter. He had stuttered in the past, but now stuttered only when he was extremely nervous. He was so terrorized at the possibility of being called on that it became a self-fulfilling prophecy. He got so anxious when the teacher called his name that, in fact, he did stutter.

Dr. Seiden reports: "We ranked his fear of stuttering if called upon in class as a 9 on a scale of 1 to 10. He tapped to: *Even though I stutter I accept myself.* He tapped all face spots and all torso spots. After he finished this tapping, and saying the sentence on each spot, he was instructed to place his hands in his lap in a relaxed fashion, close his eyes, and slowly breathe in through his nose and out through his mouth. He did this full sequence several times, until his rating fell to a 0. When he came in the next week, he said he was not afraid of participating in class. That last visit to my office was his final session."

CHILDREN AND TRAUMA

IF YOUR CHILD has had a serious trauma—hospitalization and life-threatening illness, death of a family member, car accident, physical abuse, sexual abuse—tapping will help him or her get over the emotional aspects of the ordeal.

To do a complete job of eradicating the effects of a terrifying experience, the tapping should be done on every upsetting aspect of the situation. If you can get your child to talk about it, simply repeat the negative details that are revealed, one at a time, and tap on each. One of my colleagues is the mother of Alexis, a child who benefited from her mother's knowledge of the Tapping Cure.

When Alexis, a seven-year-old girl who lived in the suburbs, was walking on her street to her best friend's house, a man in a van pulled up next to her and asked for directions. She answered him; he said he couldn't hear her and got out of the car to stand next to her. Alexis became frightened, later saying it was because he had a bad smell, and ran into her friend's home. The friend's mother chastised her for "barging in" and not waiting at the door to be admitted. Alexis called her mother and asked her to come get her. When the mother arrived, in a matter of moments, Alexis ran into her arms and sobbed. She told her everything that had happened and how frightened she was. The mother called the police to report the incident, but also put Alexis on her lap and tapped her while saying:

- *Even though the bad man spoke to you, you are OK.*
- *Even though the bad man had a bad smell you are OK.*
- *Even though you were so scared you are OK.*
- *Even though you ran into Hannah's house without knocking you are OK.*
- *Even though Hannah's mother yelled at you, you are OK.*

When the police arrived fifteen minutes later to get a description of the man and his vehicle, they were amazed at the calmness and poise of Alexis. For a moment they wondered if the incident had truly occurred. Immediate tapping saved the day. The potentially traumatic incident was neutralized, and Alexis could speak about it without any negativity; she simply stated the facts.

NO MORE TANTRUMS

YOU CAN TEACH your child to self-soothe by teaching him or her to tap. When stress threatens, instead of having a meltdown, your child will know how to get back on track. Nurse Crilly says, "Teach your kids tapping and then when they act up, instead of banishing them to their rooms, you'll say, 'go and tap yourself.'"

Remember This

CHILDREN, LIKE ADULTS, do best when they are treated respectfully. They do not do well when they are humiliated or criticized. Tapping helps you to build an alliance with your child; you are demonstrating that you are both on the same team. You and your child are cooperators, not adversaries. Figure out your child's best tapping spot, and then remind him or her to use it.

The Controversies
Surrounding Tapping

*I*F THE TAPPING Cure is so great, how come it's not sweeping the nation? Why is it that tapping techniques are not taught everywhere? How come people use tapping as a last resort after all other methods fail, instead of as their first method of treatment? How come many psychiatrists and psychologists have never heard of it? How come many medical professionals who *have* heard of it think it is nonsense?

The answer to that last question helps us know the answers to all the other questions: most health-care professionals are not willing to try tapping. If you've never tried it and simply hear that tapping on your face or hands or torso will change you instantly from a frightened driver to a relaxed, eager driver, or from a person who consistently obsesses about the past to a person who rarely thinks of the past, you, too, might think it's quackery. The doctors I know who condemn tapping as something crazy are unwilling to try it on themselves or a family member. I admit, it *does* sound weird to say that thinking about an upsetting psychological situation while at the same time tapping certain body spots will bring you swift resolution to your problem. Nevertheless, usually when someone tries it, they are hooked.

$\mathcal{W}$ise $\mathcal{W}$ords

When a true genius appears in this world,
you may know him by this sign: that the dunces
are all in confederacy against him.

—Jonathan Swift

ADOPTING NEW METHODS

LACK OF RECOGNITION for tapping therapies is disappointing, but not surprising. Normal human behavior favors accepting what is and condemning what is not. We tend to assume that useful ideas are permanent.

In 1943, IBM Chairman Thomas Watson said, "I think there is a world market for maybe five computers." And, as recently as 1977, Ken Olson, the president of Digital Equipment Corporation, speaking at the Convention of the World Future Society in Boston, said, "There is no reason for any individual to have a computer in their home."

One hundred years ago the Wright Brothers announced they had built a flying machine. They could not get anyone from the U.S. Army or the press to come out and see it. The *Scientific American Magazine* called them the Lying Brothers and refused to send a reporter. They were branded hoaxers for years. Why? Because railroads were working just fine and a new way to do things seemed preposterous. And, of course, a human enclosed within a flying machine was a scary image.

When Robert Fulton was ready to launch his steamboat, crowds watched and shouted, "He'll never get it to start." After the steamboat was chugging along, those very same naysayers were heard shouting, "He'll never get it to stop."

ᴄ𝒲ɪꜱᴇ 𝒲ᴏʀᴅꜱ

*Man's mind, stretched to a new idea, never goes
back to its original dimension.*

−Oliver Wendell Holmes

MEDICINE

MEDICINE, TOO, HAS a record of condemning new techniques.

BLOOD

In 1628, William Harvey shocked his readers by publishing a paper purporting that blood circulated within the human body. The current thinking had been that food was converted into blood by the liver and then used as fuel by the body. When Harvey explained that the heart pumped blood throughout the body and then received it back, there was an uproar; the medical community ostracized Dr. Harvey for many years.

CHILDBIRTH

Similarly, in 1847, in Vienna, when Ignaz Semmelweis instructed doctors to wash their hands before delivering babies in the hospital, he, too, was ostracized. In fact, when he suggested that doctors wash their hands after doing surgery, performing autopsies, or caring for patients with festering wounds, he was fired from his hospital job. The doctors refused to consider Semmelweis's hand-washing idea. Semmelweis had observed that when midwives delivered babies, the mothers tended to do just fine. But when doctors did the delivery, one of every six new mothers died of childbed fever. Semmelweis speculated that because the doctors had attended sick patients prior to the childbirth, perhaps childbed fever was actually an infection picked up at a sickbed and spread by the physician.

PREMATURE INFANTS

And then there was Dr. Martin Couney, a pediatrician with an unorthodox idea. At the turn of the last century, a time when neonatology was not yet a subspecialty, Couney suspected that teeny premature infants might survive if they were placed in warmed boxes. No hospital endorsed this idea; nor would any hospital permit Couney to bring his homemade equipment to their floors. Instead, parents of newborn premature babies were simply discouraged by the hospital staff from hoping for their infant's survival. Placing these babies in protected, well-regulated heated units was considered heretical. The medical establishment mockingly called Couney's setup a baby hatchery.

Dr. Couney went about building his heated baby boxes anyway. When parents despaired that their premature babies might die, Couney said he would care for them—for free. He placed the babies in his warm boxes, thus providing the most advanced treatment available for premature infants. When blocked from admittance to hospitals, Couney launched a creative solution. He established exhibits of his "babies in boxes" at fairs and amusement parks. The first was at the Victorian Era Exhibition in London, in 1897; the next year came the Trans Mississippi International Exposition in Omaha, Nebraska; and in 1903 Couney established the longest-running "freak show" in Coney Island. Trendy travelers enjoyed exhibitions that included side shows and from 1903 until 1933 visitors to Coney Island enjoyed seeing the "smallest babies on earth." Onlookers paid admission to gawk at the minuscule infants in their glass boxes, and it was the entrance fees that paid for the jerry-built incubators. Fascinated curiosity seekers regularly returned to watch the babies, rejoicing when a particular baby was finally healthy enough to go home. In 1939 the New York World's Fair had an "incubator baby side show," but it wasn't until the 1940s that hospitals finally accepted the idea of an incubator and established special units for premature babies. Although Dr. Couney saved so many lives with his bold innovation, when he died in 1950, he was poverty-stricken.

ULCERS

Even more recently, in 1983, Dr. Barry Marshall suspected that ulcers and gastritis might not be caused by stress or acid, as was then widely believed, but rather by bacteria. His laboratory studies supported his theory. However, when he presented his findings at an annual meeting of gastroenterologists, he was laughed at. Dr. Marshall was young and at the beginning of his research career. The older doctors at the meeting told him his idea was ridiculous and refused to take him seriously. Marshall, however, did not give up. In fact, he went to great lengths to prove his point. Dr. Marshall isolated the bacteria, which he called *H. pylori*, and drank it! To his delight he developed gastritis and a pre-ulcer infection. While ill, he had an imaging procedure done on himself so that his digestive tract could be examined by his peers. In 1995 Dr. Marshall received the prestigious Lasker Award. In 2005 he won the Nobel Prize for discovering *H. pylori*.

ᑲᎳ𝗜𝗦𝗘 ᑲᎳᎾᖇᗪ𝗦

If at first the idea is not absurd,
then there is no hope for it.

—Albert Einstein

SKEPTICS

JUST AS THE ideas of circulating blood, hand-washing, and warmed baby boxes were thought to be strange, so, too, the idea of energy psychology, with its effort to change emotions without psychological dialogue, seems incredible to some people. And those very people are not impressed by the research. It is true that although research has been done, it has not been rigorous. Most of the evidence of success is anecdotal, and scientists are not impressed by anecdotal evidence. You, of course, are impressed if the anecdote is about you. If you are the person described in the anecdotal report and you are suddenly symptom-free, you know the value of tapping without the endorsement of the medical establishment. There are many, many satisfied tappers, yet they are not part of a medical cohort scrutinized by all the proper authorities

It is possible that we will need a new paradigm—a new way of evaluating the success of a treatment. In traditional science, success is measured by comparing two different interventions and observing that the outcome of one is superior to the outcome of the other. The interventions are conducted on subjects who are suffering from similar symptoms, the details of which are clearly known and measured. We know about the process that creates change and we understand the scientific explanations. In tapping we consider an intervention to be a success when, prior to tapping, the person is in distress and, after tapping, that same person is feeling great. Whereas that should be good enough to applaud, it does not follow any known research model. Energy therapists who are honest will admit that their treatment does not make sense according to the laboratory and according to the world of molecules. It may be that at this point in time we simply don't know the standard needed to study tapping. But we do know that tapping works.

When a permanent cure for a problem or symptom that was impossible to cure before appears, there is reason both to rejoice and to question. The question is, "What is going on here?" and the answer is, "We don't know." We don't know the science of the success of tapping, even though we do know it is successful. Most medical professionals are not willing to risk their reputation and the respect of their colleagues by endorsing a controversial technique. However, that said, know that the Association of Energy Psychology, an international organization for researchers and practitioners, had just over 500 members in 2002, yet in 2005 boasts a membership of 781. That's progress!

ꞯISE ꞯORDS

Most men occasionally stumble over the truth,
but most pick themselves up and continue on
as if nothing happened.

—Winston Churchill

There are some skeptics who do not believe in the effectiveness of tapping. They see a clinician's reports of success and say it is not understandable, because there is no psychotherapeutic relationship; there is no cognitive reorganization; there is no reward system in place; there is no insight. I've also heard some critics concede that they've seen a cure in a patient but doubt that the cure will last forever. I'm not sure that is a valid criticism. The effect rarely, in my experience, wears off. But, if it should, the person need only tap again to get the same good results. And, in fairness, I've never heard mainstream medical folks become alarmed when a patient recovers from a cold. I've not heard them say the cure is worthless because next winter the patient may sneeze again.

THE FRINGE

To make matters worse, any time you are dealing with fringe science you must deal with the fringe scientists who are attracted to it. I was at a professional meeting where a tapping guru accomplished wonders during a demonstration with an audience volunteer, but then lost all credibility when he said, "Oh, this method is so successful it not only cures phobias, as you just witnessed, but it can also cure multiple sclerosis." His ridiculous statement turned off many of the professionals who just a few moments earlier had been eager to learn more about tapping. As Carl Sagan said, "Some geniuses have been laughed at, but not all who are laughed at are geniuses."

SEMANTICS

ANOTHER TURNOFF IS the vocabulary that some energy psychologists have developed. Dr. Callahan, the granddaddy of the tapping methods and founder and developer of Thought Field Therapy, defines the *thought field* as an invisible structure in space that has an effect on matter. He calls the sequence of his tapping spots *algorithms,* and when one of his patients does not succeed right away he says that a *perturbation* has caused a negative emotion. If a client is cured but attributes the cure to something other than the tapping, Dr. Callahan calls that an *apex* problem. Traditional scientists have trouble accepting these terms; it's easier and more inviting to speak simply, using a familiar vocabulary.

Wise Words

Every inventor is a crackpot until his idea succeeds.

—Mark Twain

PLACEBOS

IF I CLAIM that tapping will cure stage fright and then I proceed to tap ten people and nine of them are no longer afraid of performing on stage, may I declare tapping a cure for stage fright? Maybe. It certainly appears that way. But maybe it was the placebo effect. Maybe the expectation of change produced change. Maybe there was nothing about the actual tapping that contributed to the cure.

When a neutral substance, something that has no power of its own, produces a positive change, we call that change the placebo effect. The *something* that is responsible for the change could be words, could be a pill, could be a thought, or could be a physical action such as tapping. Some people think the success of tapping comes not from the tapping per se, but from the placebo effect.

Placebo is a Latin word taken from the Catholic prayer for the dead. It means, "I shall please." The placebo effect is a blessing. It is your body's way of turning something neutral into something helpful. If you heal as a result of the placebo effect, you are indeed lucky.

A placebo is considered neutral only when it is by itself. When the placebo substance is absorbed by your mind or by your body at just the right point in time, it becomes a potent remedy. Although it has no curative powers of its own, it mobilizes you to have a good response to whatever treatment you are being given.

You might be interested to know that there is also a term called *nocebo*. Words or neutral substances that create a negative effect on your body are called nocebos. A typical nocebo is the insert in the package containing your medicine when you get your drugs from the pharmacy. Upon reading that folded-up white paper with small print that tells you all the horrors that could befall you, you may just "happen" to develop one of the enumerated side effects.

If a placebo works for you, it really makes a change in you. It's not all in your mind. You are not imagining a change. The placebo effect creates a physiologic change. Your mind is powerful and your mind takes that harmless, inert placebo substance and converts it into a healing substance.

Before a new drug or a new procedure or a new treatment method is permitted to be incorporated into the standard of care, it must be tested. The National Institutes of Health (NIH) and the National Institute of Mental Health (NIMH), as well as private pharmaceutical companies and research universities, conduct many, many medical tests with placebos every year. Prior to a treatment being declared safe and effective, it must be tried out on a respectable number of people, called *subjects.* The results are carefully monitored and recorded.

If I wanted to run a valid test of the tapping method, in addition to my original ten subjects described above who have stage fright,

I would need to locate an additional ten subjects who also have stage fright. For these latter subjects I would choose one or two or three spots that are not tapping spots. I would pretend that those sham spots were the spots for eliminating stage fright. I would then proceed to tap and say whatever sentences I had said with the previous group. When the results were tallied, we'd see how many were cured. If none of those who were tapped on phony tapping spots were cured, then we'd know that the true tapping spots have validity. If a couple of subjects were cured, we'd know they were cured by the placebo effect. If nine out of ten were cured, it would make the case for the tapping spots rather weak.

As mentioned above, we don't have sufficient scientific evidence that tapping is as powerful as it seems to be. The evidence we do have is anecdotal. That is, mental health professionals can talk about many, many clients and patients whom we have tapped and helped.

Dr. Steven Jay Lynn is a professor of psychology at SUNY Binghamton. He is a serious scientist, and he has said, "Anecdotal evidence is never 'good enough.'" It is, however, a starting point for more rigorous studies, and can suggest hypotheses that can be examined by methodologically sound, controlled studies with random assignment of subjects to treatment groups. I would not be convinced by anecdotal reports because many patients do, in fact, report short-term gains as a result of virtually any psychotherapeutic intervention, and there are serious selection biases in people who report they are helped. That is, we generally don't hear from individuals who are not helped. That's why we need well-controlled studies, with random assignment of clients to groups, and long-term follow-ups. On the other hand, anecdotal reports do pique my curiosity, and often prod me to learn much more about a particular approach than might otherwise be the case.

ᵂISE ᵂORDS

*Creativity requires the courage to
let go of certainties.*

—Erich Fromm

HEALERS

ANOTHER HYPOTHESIS TO account for the success of tapping is the natural healing ability of the person doing the tapping. Might it be possible that some people are healers and whatever they do to an ill person will help that person get better? Healers may have soothing voices than calm agitated patients, or they may have some unknown quality within them that helps a patient mobilize inner resources and begin the healing process. Some people react with good health when they simply feel understood. For decades, psychotherapists have helped patients feel understood. Might feeling understood begin a curing process? Maybe. Science does not yet know or recognize person-to-person healing without use of medication or standard treatment protocols.

NEW RESEARCH

SOME RECENT RESEARCH showing the efficacy of tapping has been published in the *Journal of Clinical Psychology*. This is a start toward acceptance by the establishment, but there's a hitch. Dr. Callahan, whose work is reviewed in the scholarly journal, forbade other psychologists to review his papers. He said that they would not treat him fairly because they were prejudiced against his type of research. This is peculiar, because academic journals are supposed to publish only research that is peer-reviewed. If Callahan doesn't permit a professional peer to review his work, it becomes suspect. Yet, there *is* so much prejudice against him that he might have a point. It's an interesting dilemma.

There are several research studies now going on which thus far have promising results. The road ahead is difficult, though. When Professor Charles Figley, of Florida State University, compared several therapies for the treatment of trauma, he concluded that tapping, and Thought Field Therapy in particular, "is extraordinarily powerful, can be taught to nearly anyone, appears to do no harm, does not require the clients to talk about their troubles, and is fast and long-lasting." The psychiatric establishment chastised him for not using appropriate clinical trials and not using appropriate research methodology. They forgot to notice that the clients being treated got better and had stayed that way when they were checked up on many months later. So, it seems that while anecdotal evidence may be enough to convince clients, professionals rightfully need scientifically controlled tests in order to accept a new method.

Dr. John Diepold Jr. successfully uses tapping in his practice and says, "There is no empirical evidence from experimental studies to establish that it is the tapping that works in the treatment of psychological problems. . . . Tapping does work, as evidenced in clinical treatment and the multitude of anecdotal reports and patient testimonials . . . the time has come to empirically validate the tapping approach. . . ."

Wise Words

An important scientific innovation rarely makes its way by gradually winning over and converting its opponents. What does happen is that the opponents gradually die out.

—Nobel Prize winner Max Planck

TAPPING CONTROVERSIES

WITHIN THE VARIOUS schools and philosophies of tapping there are several issues that cannot be agreed upon, including muscle testing, sequencing, and surrogate tapping. This in-fighting, and a lack of a united front, may be responsible for some of the resistance to tapping by the mainstream. It's not important to your cure that you know about these procedural differences. You can easily follow the instructions of previous chapters and accomplish whatever you set out to. The ideas discussed below are presented simply to satisfy your intellectual curiosity about the process.

MUSCLE TESTING

Kinesiology is the study of the science of body mechanics and muscle function and movement. Applied kinesiology is the study of muscles and muscle strength. Chiropractors tend to support the use of applied kinesiology far more than do physicians. It is a controversial field of study founded by George Goodheart, a Detroit chiropractor, back in the 1960s. Goodheart's method is essentially a feedback procedure that determines how well or how poorly the patient's body is functioning. Dr. Goodheart's examinations are rigorous and complex, and his testing of muscles helps him come up with a diagnosis for his patients.

Some of the principles of applied kinesiology prompted psychologist Roger Callahan to investigate methods of detecting imbalances in the body and the mind, and of then reestablishing a harmonious, symptom-free level of functioning, all of which led to Thought Field Therapy.

Applied kinesiology, like energy psychology, assumes that blocked energy creates imbalances, which then cause symptoms. Some energy psychologists have decided to use muscle testing, in their own fashion, to determine what is really bothering their patient. To those therapists, muscle testing becomes the mechanical equivalent of a truth serum. Most of the muscle testing done by tappers is not as extensive as the muscle testing done by Dr. Goodheart; nevertheless, the practitioners insist that they get excellent results from tapping thanks to the prior muscle testing procedures.

Here's how it works: Practitioners ask their patient to concentrate on the distressing situation from which they want relief and simultaneously extend their arm out at shoulder height. The practitioner then tries to push down on the arm. The theory is that if the patient is being truthful and really wants relief from that situation, the arm muscles will be strong and the arm will not budge. But if the patient has some unconscious conflict, that conflict will weaken the muscle and the practitioner will easily push down the arm. By asking many questions and trying to push down the subject's arm whenever he or she gives an answer, it is hoped that the many layers of the problem to be worked on will be revealed. Using the additional information gleaned from muscle testing, when a tapping sentence is formulated it will include the most accurate words.

Try It on a Friend

Ask your friend to extend his arm, keeping it either out front or to the side, at shoulder height. Then tell him to hold it taut and not permit you to move it when you push down on it. Then tell him to utter a truthful statement—for example, today is Thursday—and again attempt to push his arm down. Probably, you won't be able to. Next, ask your friend to utter a false statement—for example, today is Sunday—and again attempt to push down his arm. Probably the arm will easily move down. The theory is that muscles weaken when there is conflict between what is said and the truth.

Try It on Yourself

With the thumb and middle finger of one hand make a circle. Do the same with your other hand, but first put your thumb through the first hand's circle. Now you have two interlocking loops. Pull the linked fingers of one hand against those of the other. Hold your fingers firmly in a circle so that your loop will not be broken. Now say aloud a truthful statement while one hand tries to separate the fingers of the other hand. Resist. Don't break the loop. Good. Now, say aloud a false statement—for example, it's raining outside (use this only if it's sunny)—and again try with one hand to separate the fingers of the other. Resist. Does the loop break anyway? For many people saying an untruth weakens their muscles and they cannot sustain their finger loop. For some, though, this works only when someone else does it to them, not when they administer the muscle testing to themselves.

Muscle Testing and Tapping

Some tapping practitioners prefer to include muscle testing as part of their procedure. They believe that only through muscle testing do they know precisely what the true core issues are and which meridians are most important to tap on. They believe they can determine the truth by asking questions such as, "Do you really want this symptom to go away?" or "Does that abuse memory have something to do with your brother and not a stranger?" They believe, too, that by detecting weakness in a particular muscle they can determine precisely where to tap, because according to their theory every muscle corresponds to a particular meridian.

Some tapping therapists use muscle testing all the time and some, like me, do not. I am not convinced that it leads to a faster or better Tapping Cure. Sometimes I use it when trying to help a cynical person—it's usually a young man—get rid of a serious problem. When he responds well to muscle testing, he is convinced that I might know something he doesn't and he'll be more receptive to the Tapping Cure.

SEQUENCING

Some practitioners of tapping believe that every problem that a client has can be tapped away with a particular formula. The formula, often called a recipe or an algorithm, is a specific sequence of tapping spots. For example, according to some doctors fear of flying can be eradicated by tapping on Under-Eye, Collarbone, Side, and then V. The clients are instructed to tap those spots only, and in that particular order. These doctors have lists of formulas, each corresponding to a particular malady. Also, as part of the sequence, some tapping practitioners insist that their clients do the full 9 Gamut treatment, as described in chapter 8. Other tapping gurus advise all clients to tap on every tapping spot, no matter their symptoms. And still others say, "Pick a couple of spots and tap on them. It makes no difference which spots or in which order."

In my experience, clients come to know which of their tapping spots are most useful to them. Throughout this book I have urged you to pay attention and try to figure out which spots your body and your mind best respond to. When you tap on the spots that you've identified as most helpful they will work for you in many situations, not just one or two. I believe that tapping spots are determined by the person, not the situation. Thus, the same spots would work for you to help you recover from a trauma and to prepare you for a public speaking event. That said, when I've had many clients report that one particular tapping spot works best for one particular problem, for example the Mustache spot for shyness, I enthusiastically pass along that information to you—in the form of a Hot Spot heads-up. It's something else for you to try. You are unique, and you will be your best healer.

Monica Pignotti, an early advocate of Thought Field Therapy, and someone who has spent much time and money studying with Dr. Callahan, has now renounced sequencing. In her experiments, patients who tapped on random spots did just as well as those who tapped on prescribed spots. Again, it's up to you to figure out which tapping technique best suits you.

Sometimes I've wondered whether or not the words that are spoken at the very moment that the troublesome thought is aroused to consciousness might be an important part of the cure. But just when I think the tapping doesn't matter as much as the words, I'll have a client who simply taps without speaking and immediately sees results. So we just don't yet know what it is that creates the change in a person who simultaneously thinks about and speaks about a disturbing thought while also tapping on particular points.

DIAGNOSING

I AM A believer in tapping *and* I am a believer in traditional medication and traditional medical practices. The two are not mutually exclusive. I do not believe that tapping is the cure for everything. When a client comes into my office asking for pain relief, I know very well I can diminish their pain, but I won't. I will insist on speaking to their physician to find out whether or not the pain is a signal that something needs to be attended to. I will not tap away leg pain without an X-ray to make sure that there is not a broken bone; I will not tap away a headache until we know why the headache occurred. I believe in obtaining a diagnosis for physical conditions. Within the field of tapping, there are practitioners who think they can get at the underlying cause of every ailment, and some of those practitioners are not physicians and not psychologists and have neither the medical ability nor the legal consent to diagnose. So be careful.

RELATIONSHIPS

WHEN CLIENTS COME to my office wanting help with relationship issues, I do not always prescribe the Tapping Cure. I believe that couples should first address their differences in communication styles and in intimacy levels, and also some of the habits that each formed years ago in their families of origin. They can do this in one or two sessions with a good marriage counselor or a well-trained religious leader, or maybe a good friend or family member. There's always time to tap later.

SURROGATE TAPPING

SOME TAPPING PROFESSIONALS insist that they've attained good results by tapping on a surrogate, not the patient! I've read accounts of tappers tapping on themselves, tapping on a stuffed animal, tapping on a doll, and tapping on a third person.

When I voice my skepticism and say, "You are one of the folks who give tapping a bad name," they justify their actions by claiming that their results are good. One such practitioner said, "When I pray for someone's health they can be far away. Surrogate tapping is just another form of distance healing via prayer." This remains an area of controversy. Earlier we spoke of the fringe. Please be informed that there are folks who earn a living tapping on dogs. They insist that tapping changes the dogs' disposition.

REVERSALS AND POLARITY

SOME ENERGY PSYCHOLOGISTS believe that the body's energy has both negative and positive poles and that symptoms are produced when the polarity becomes reversed. The reversed polarity is what is responsible for disturbing thoughts and disturbed behavior. When the polarity is reversed, it is believed, tapping will not work and the symptoms will persist. However, correcting the polarity is possible by tapping on the Karate spot or rubbing the Pledge spot. Not every practitioner endorses this. Plenty of well-educated health professionals do not believe negative and positive poles exist within the human body. I decided to include those two tapping spots in my regular sequence of spots in an effort to be as efficient as possible. Reversal or self-sabotaging polarity may or may not exist, and if they don't, well, we've wasted only a minute of our time. There's no need for a lengthy dialogue or investigation. If there is a possibility that tapping and rubbing those spots will help you heal, it seems counterproductive not to suggest using them. And perhaps they do help you heal—for reasons having nothing to do with polarity and everything to do with something that we've not yet figured out.

TALKING

SOME TAPPING PRACTITIONERS advocate silence; others prefer that religious affirmations be chanted during tapping; and still others want a single key word spoken. I like to have my clients say a full affirming sentence for the first two tapping spots, in fact the very spots that have the capacity to reverse a polarity—if there is one— and then to say just one or two key words for the other spots. I find that I need not be doctrinaire; clients tap and decide for themselves whether to say a full sentence or a key word. Similarly, they decide for themselves whether to tap with their eyes open or closed. I mention nothing about the eyes, yet some clients automatically close their eyes, and that's just fine.

DO-IT-YOURSELF?

THERE ARE PLENTY of people who will happily accept your money in exchange for tapping on your body. I recommend that you tap yourself. After all, in the comfort of your home, the convenience is there and the price is right. You are not stupid. If you encounter a problem, you will consult a therapist. If your circumstances are extremely complex, you may need a tapping practitioner to sort out your many issues and help you come up with all the sentences to tap on. However, most of the time, for most people, do-it-yourself works.

For some people, tapping represents a form of touching, and touching can be a sign of dominance. If one person is dominant, then the other automatically is subservient or submissive. In our society it's most often adults who touch children, employers who touch employees, a man who touches a woman. For example, the male accountant may paternalistically put his hands upon his secretary's shoulder; the female accountant will do no such thing. The adult may touch the child's head in an affectionate pat; the child will not reach up and reciprocate. If you are sensitive about the issue of touching, that is another reason for you to tap yourself and maintain your dignity.

The results of tapping are so spectacular that it won't be long before it is more widely accepted. Just think, you will have been there at the inception—one of the pioneers. Good for you!

Remember This

ONLY YOU CAN determine the effects of tapping. If you feel better, then you have succeeded. Don't let anyone persuade you that because it is not yet a scientifically validated procedure, you should stop using it. You are in charge of your body and you are in charge of your mind. If you don't feel better, seek help elsewhere. You are entitled to be symptom-free.

Who's Who
in the Tapping World

*I*T'S NOT EASY to keep track of tapping theorists. They often use letters of the alphabet to represent their techniques, and the result is an alphabet soup. If you are intrigued and want to learn more about tapping, please follow the trails begun in this chapter. The information below should help ease your way through the various methods and familiarize you with TFT, EFT, TAB, TAT, and the rest of the tapping alphabet soup.

WHO'S WHO

Roger Callahan, PhD, is the person who created Thought Field Therapy (TFT). He is the director of the Thought Field Therapy Training Center in La Quinta, California, publisher of the quarterly newsletter *The Thought Field*, and chairman of the board of the professional organization Association for Thought Field Therapy. TFT is often considered the original tapping therapy and involves specific tapping sequences as well as Callahan's 9 Gamut tapping technique, which includes eye movements, humming, and counting. Callahan's most popular book—he's written many—is *Tapping the Healer Within: Using*

Thought Field Therapy to Instantly Conquer Your Fears, Anxieties, and Emotional Distress.

Callahan goes beyond mere tapping and also advocates a method of diagnosis using the voice of the client. He prescribes individualized treatment sequences for every possible problem. For a hefty fee, Callahan will instruct therapists in the use of his methods and share certain therapeutic secrets with them. You can learn more about TFT at http://www.tftrx.com and you can contact Dr. Callahan directly at roger@tftrx.com. His Web site includes interesting case studies from his practice.

Gary Craig is the creator of the Emotional Freedom Techniques (EFT), which is based upon Thought Field Therapy and influenced by Neuro-Linguistic Programming (NLP, a communication method that claims to enhance information processing and is based upon the theory that we filter all events and words according to our own biases and thus distort the truth. NLP practitioners teach ways to communicate with clarity and improve relationships). Craig is a Stanford engineering graduate and an ordained minister. He is self-taught in energy psychology and not formally trained in psychology or psychotherapy. He brings a spiritual perspective to tapping. Craig believes his technique is easier to follow than Thought Field Therapy because he does not use different spots for different situations, but instead, like the Tapping Cure, recommends that all spots be tapped. Craig's Web site, http://www.emofree.com, is full, generous, and amazingly comprehensive. It is thoughtfully organized and provides a straightforward and detailed description of exactly what Emotional Freedom Technique is and what it can be used to treat. There is a free, downloadable, seventy-nine-page EFT manual that explains the underlying theory and mechanics of performing EFT. In his section called "EFT Cousins," you can link to even more energy psychology Web sites. Craig has included tutorials, workshops, and plenty of inspiration on his site.

John Diamond, MD, is one of the energy psychology pioneers. In 1979, Diamond developed behavioral kinesiology, which incorporated ideas from psychiatry and psychotherapy as well as music and the humanities. Later he expanded his techniques and renamed his method "Life-Energy Analysis." He believes that an imbalance of a "Vital Force" can affect a specific energy meridian and lead to psychological and physical problems. He has conducted experiments on the effect of negative thinking and believes that mind and body continually interact. One of his books is *Life Energy—Using the Meridians to Unlock the Hidden Power of Your Emotions.* Learn more about Diamond at www.diamondcenter.net.

John H. Diepold Jr. is the inventor of Touch and Breathe (TAB). He asserts that touching the acupoint spot but not tapping on it works well if you take a good deep breath while doing so. Then you move on to the next tapping spot, touch it (don't tap), and again take a deliberate breath. Diepold is a bit academic when he uses jargon such as: "In TAB, the use of one complete respiration (one easy inhalation and exhalation) is the natural vehicle of Chi circulation, which also creates a piezoelectric effect via vibration and sound (sonic resonance)." This sound is believed to have a calming effect on the patient. Diepold continues, "It appears that the natural motion and sound of the breathing process creates a powerful energetic influence involving the piezoelectric response mechanism. The radiation of this energy conceivably enhances the antenna/transmitter function of the body as it is directed to the specific acupuncture points by way of sustained touch." Breathing never sounded so complicated, but Diepold's theories are interesting and useful, nevertheless. You can learn more about TAB from Diepold's interesting and informative Web site, www.tftworldwide.com/tab.html, and in his book, *Evolving Thought Field Therapy: The Clinician's Handbook of Diagnoses, Treatment, and Theory.*

Tapas Fleming began her therapeutic work as an acupuncturist. Her method, called Tapas Acupressure Technique (TAT), is surprisingly easy to do. You simply place your fingertips on three specific points near your eyes with one hand, and with the other hand you press the base of your skull. This is called the TAT pose. There is no tapping and there are no strong emotions brought up. It is a peaceful healing technique that has a strong spiritual/religious component. While maintaining the pose, you are to say aloud several prescribed statements. TAT focuses on only a few acupuncture points, all having to do with vision. Tapas believes you must "see" past trauma to overcome it. Her book, *You Can Heal Now: The Tapas Acupressure Technique (TAT) Workbook*, can be downloaded from her Web site: www.tatlife.com and/or tat-intl.com. The Web site gives detailed instructions on how to use the technique and talks about ways to heal yourself from allergies and from PTSD.

Fred P. Gallo, PhD, was among the first professionals to have studied TFT with Dr. Callahan. Gallo also studied with Dr. John Diamond, founder of behavioral kinesiology. Gallo is a psychologist who claims to have coined the term energy psychology. He is the author of several books, including *Energy Diagnostic and Treatment Methods, Energy Tapping,* and his latest, *Energy Psychology in Psychotherapy.* He trains therapists throughout the world and has added some of his own tapping points to those of Dr. Callahan. One of Gallo's methods is called EDxTM, which stands for Energy Diagnostic and Treatment Methods. He practices in Hermitage, Pennsylvania. On his Web site, http://www.energypsych.com, you can find articles he's written about studies related to energy psychology. Gallo attempts to avoid New Age jargon as much as possible while describing his method, which he says incorporates principles from applied kinesiology, bioenergy, consciousness, and cognition.

Gregory Nicosia, PhD, is the developer of a tapping technique that is similar to TFT and is reliant upon muscle testing. Nicosia is a licensed psychologist and the founder of Advanced Diagnostics, P.C., a center for the "thought energy based psychotherapeutic treatment of trauma and remediation of cognitive dysfunction" in Pittsburgh, Pennsylvania. His Web site is www.thoughtenergy.com. In the Questions and Answers section of this site, you'll find an interesting letter from a rather traditional physician who talks about his surprisingly successful experience with tapping.

Larry Nims is the originator of Be Set Free Fast (BSFF), his personal take on TFT. His practice is in Orange, California, and he has experience as a university teacher, clinical supervisor, and consultant. Nims says BSFF differs from other energy therapies by focusing on the unconscious mind and the unresolved emotional conflicts hidden within it. He is concerned with the belief systems that exist behind problems—particularly fears, anger, sadness, and trauma. Nims's book, *Be Set Free Fast: Release Your Discomforts Now* is available through his Web site, http://www.besetfreefast.com.

Monica Pignotti is a social worker and psychotherapist who once was a follower of Callahan's TFT (and paid the required tuition to learn his advanced techniques). Since then, however, Pignotti has conducted some experiments that she believes prove that there is a fallacy in Callahan's methods. She's written several articles on why she no longer believes in TFT Voice Technology (VT), and has had a peer-reviewed study accepted for publication that she says proves TFT VT "does no better than randomly selected treatment points." Her blog is a must-read for skeptics and followers alike: http://psychjourney_blogs.typepad.com/monica_pignotti_/.

Steve Reed, a psychotherapist, developed a process called REMAP, which is yet another twist on the energy psychologies. His Web site, www.psychotherapy-center.com, is excellent, with interesting articles and solid information. According to Reed, research has proved that specific acupressure points produce specific results in particular areas of the brain. The REMAP process uses all 361 of the traditional Chinese acupoints in a precise method that allows a practitioner to determine which meridians need to be treated and which points along the meridian require treatment. Reed says he can do this without muscle testing. He also claims his method is easily taught, because he has devised REMAP acupressure charts that make it unnecessary to memorize any of the acupoints. Using seven steps, REMAP systematically identifies and treats multiple aspects of a presenting problem. Systematically working each point along the meridian that holds the most intensity, Reed claims to identify and uncover hidden layers of emotional problems.

WISE WORDS

The greatest discovery of my generation is
that a human being can alter his life by altering
his attitudes of mind.

—William James

ADDITIONAL RELEVANT WEB SITES

INSIDE THE UNITED STATES

www.energypsych.org

This is the Web site for the Association for Comprehensive Energy Psychology (ACEP). This site serves as the online persona of the professional organization for practitioners of energy psychology. Its goal is to promote "professional energy psychology and collaboration among practitioners, researchers, and licensing bodies."

Although it's aimed at therapists and scholars, there's plenty of good, easily understandable information for everyone. You can learn about ACEP-sponsored research, read the texts of various professional articles about energy psychology, and participate in home-study continuing ed classes and classes by telephone. There are book reviews and listings of independent (i.e., non-ACEP-affiliated) EP workshops, nationally and internationally. In addition to collecting disparate information about energy psychology, this site provides links to many other resources.

www.the-tree-of-life.com

Attractor Field Technique (AFT) is yet another energy psychology, this one based upon the work of David R. Hawkins, MD, PhD, and the author of *Power vs. Force: The Hidden Determinants of Human Behavior*. Hawkins gets into dubious territory by making extraordinary claims with no scientific backup. He says, "We think that we live by forces we control, but in fact we are governed by power from unrevealed sources, power over which we have *no* control." Hawkins believes he knows the truth and claims that the AFT tapping technique can cure both emotional and physical illness. He insists that daily tapping according to his particular formula is the only way to insure freedom from invisible disease-causing forces. He recommends very specific tapping sequences for addictions and for physical ailments. If you wish to try tapping according to his plan, please remember there has not been any scientific validation of it, so do not give up your medications or other treatments.

www.jmt-jafmeltechnique.com

The Jaffe-Mellor Technique is an energy psychology that uses tapping and muscle testing to treat chronic degenerative physical diseases. The founders of this method are Carolyn Jaffe, PhD, and Judy Mellor, RN, PhD, both of whom have practiced acupuncture and alternative medicine in their offices in Wyomissing, Pennsylvania, for many years. While there are many testimonials and anecdotal reports, as well as published articles on their Web site, please don't give up your traditional medications unless your physician advises you to do so.

OUTSIDE THE UNITED STATES

Tapping techniques are accepted treatments for many emotional issues and psychological problems in other parts of the world. Below you'll find Web site information from England and from New Zealand.

www.theamt.com

The Association for Meridian Energy Therapies (AMT) Web site describes itself as a portal to EP information and thus is extremely busy and somewhat overwhelming. It does have a primer on Meridian Energy Therapies (METs) for clients, and also provides information for therapists on how to get certified as an "AMT Trainer." It has links to some articles on METs that might be useful to scholars as well as clients and therapists. The AMT is based in England; thus, the practitioners and trainers recommended are based in England. Also available here are EP discussion groups and a "reviews" section that provides "testimonials, recommendations, stories, and case studies about meridian energy therapies, books, trainers, originators, and courses." Among the many links is one with numerous articles about EFT, including "The Evolution of EFT from TFT," by Gary Craig.

www.behaviourchanges.com

This Web site introduces New Zealanders to the tapping methods of EFT and provides interesting, informative articles. Read the introduction and then click on any of the titles of papers that look interesting. This Web site announces a clinical trial, sponsored by a government organization and a cancer society, that will test the efficacy of tapping in a smoking-cessation program. It is a double-blind study and the hope is that it will legitimatize tapping.

LOOKING FOR MORE?

There are myriad other Web sites related to tapping. There are chat rooms, individual blogs, informal e-mail discussion groups, and Listservs devoted to tapping. An Internet search at yahoo.com for "health groups" comes up with a couple of TFT-related e-mail discussion groups. There are anti-tapping and anti–energy psychology groups on the Internet, too. Also, there are relevant individual postings, such as www.energypsychologyintro.com.

Remember This

THE INFORMATION CONTAINED in this book can help you achieve peace of mind. You can tap into the calmness and serenity that exist within you. Relief is literally in your hands. But reading this book is not sufficient; you must also tap!

Appendix A
Tapping Spots for the Tapping Cure

Eyebrow One: at intersection of eyebrow and nose
Eyebrow Two: on temples
Under-Eye: on bony ridge under eye
Mustache: under nose
Chin: on indentation above chin
Karate: bone on side of hand used in a karate chop
V: beginning between pinkie and ring finger and extending down
　　back of hand
Pinkie: at intersection of nail and little finger
Index: at intersection of nail and index finger
Thumb: at intersection of nail and thumb
Middle: at intersection of nail and middle finger
Collarbone: on and under collarbone
Side: in between underarm and waist
Pledge:　left side of chest, under collarbone

Appendix B

Sentence Endings for the Tapping Cure

THE WORDING OF your sentence is crucial to your success. Please try various sentence endings until you find the perfect one for you and your situation.

SENTENCE ENDINGS

Your sentence endings can be simple:

- *I'm OK*
- *I'm a success*
- *I accept myself*

Or, your sentence endings can be a bit more dramatic:

- *I'm a winner*
- *I can handle it*
- *I know the truth now*
- *I don't care about that anymore*
- *I have overcome it*

Choose any phrase that will work for you and your particular situation. Here are some other suggestions:

- *It's no big deal*

- *I have a good life ahead of me*
- *I am looking ahead, not back*
- *I have no interest in that*
- *I'm in charge of myself now*
- *That was in the past*
- *I'll soon be over it*
- *I forgive myself*
- *I'm on to bigger and better things*
- *I've grown from it*
- *It is unimportant to me today*

Appendix C
Quick-Fix Chart

*J*F YOU ARE like most people, you eliminate your symptoms best when you go through a full tapping sequence, tapping on every spot. Some people, though, have identified a couple of tapping spots that always work for them and they no longer need the full sequence. Here is a list of all the tapping spots used in the Tapping Cure and the issues for which most people find them effective. You, of course, are unique. Which combinations of these work for you? Please develop your own individualized formula.

EYEBROW ONE	trauma, rejection, frustration, impatience
EYEBROW TWO	rage
UNDER-EYE	anxiety, tension, rejection, obsession, phobia, performance anxiety
MOUSTACHE	embarrassment, unworthiness
CHIN	shame
KARATE	unworthiness, sadness
V	loneliness, sadness
PINKIE	anger
INDEX	guilt

Appendic C: Quick-Fix Chart

MIDDLE	jealousy
THUMB	intolerance, impatience
COLLARBONE	trauma, rejection, loneliness, shame, jealousy, rage, guilt, embarrassment, sadness, obsession, anger, phobia, performance anxiety, anxiety, insecurity
SIDE	rejection, jealousy, phobia, performance anxiety, anxiety, tension, lack of self-confidence

Index

CPSIA information can be obtained
at www.ICGtesting.com
Printed in the USA
LVOW12s0638221016

509721LV00005B/8/P